Indian Uprising on the Rio Grande

Indian Uprising on the Rio Grande

The Pueblo Revolt of 1680

FRANKLIN FOLSOM

Introduction by Alfonso Ortiz

Chapter illustrations by J.D. Roybal

University of New Mexico Press
Albuquerque

University of New Mexico Press edition reprinted
1996 by arrangement with Franklin Folsom

21 20 19 18 17 16   8 9 10 11 12 13
ISBN-13: 978-0-8263-1743-8

The song on page 125 (adapted from "Song by Deer Katsina")
is reproduced by permission of the American Anthropological
Association from *Memiors of the American Anthropological
Association*, No. 60, Yr. 1942.

Library of Congress Cataloging-in-Publication Data
Folsom, Franklin, 1907–
  [Red power on the Rio Grande]
  Indian uprising on the Rio Grande: the Pueblo Revolt of 1680 /
Franklin Folsom; introduction by Alfonso Ortiz; chapter
illustrations by J. D. Roybal.
p.cm.
Originally published: Chicago: Follett Pub. Co., [1973]
Includes bibliographical references (p.   ) and index.

ISBN: 0-8263-1743-X (pa)

1. Pueblo Revolt, 1680.
2. Pueblo Indians—History—17th century.
I. Title.
E99.P9F64 1996
976.4'401—dc20

Contents

Acknowledgments   7

People and Indian Gods Mentioned
   in This Book   9

Introduction by *Alfonso Ortiz*   13

1/ Call to Revolution   21

2/ Aztlán Before 1680   36

3/ Crisis   52

4/ Popé   59

5/ Popé Becomes a Leader   71

6/ Choosing the Time   83

7/ Rebellion in the North   92

8/ Rebellion Far from the Center   103

9/ Siege   109

10/ Freedom   122

11/ A New Balance   126

Afterword   131

A Guide to Place Names   134

Pronunciation Guide   136

Sources   137

Index   141

Acknowledgments

For helpful consultations and letters and for reading my manuscript, I am exceedingly grateful to Dr. Alfonso Ortiz, Associate Professor of Anthropology at Princeton University, who is a Tewa from San Juan Pueblo, the home of Popé, the most important leader of the 1680 revolution.

In addition to being indebted to the publications listed on pages 137-140, I received generous help from the following:

Margaret Currier, Librarian, Peabody Museum, Harvard University; Virginia Jennings, Librarian of the Southwest and Rare Book Room of the Library of New Mexico; Dr. John Polich,

Head of the History Department, Library of the Historical Society of New Mexico; Mrs. J. K. Shishkin, History Library, Museum of New Mexico.

For valuable suggestions about the manuscript I owe special thanks to Bertha Jenkinson and Meta Smith, my editors at Follett Publishing Company, and to two careful critics—my son Dr. Michael Folsom of the Massachusetts Institute of Technology, and my wife Mary Elting Folsom.

People and Indian Gods Mentioned in This Book

Blue Corn Woman, the supernatural being who the Tewas believe is the mother of the Summer People

Brother Andrés Durán, Franciscan missionary in Water Gap (San Ildefonso)

Nicolás Bua, son-in-law of Popé and Spanish-appointed governor (tuyo) of Grinding Stone (San Juan)

Catiti, a Keres, possibly half-Spanish, of Kewa (Santo Domingo)

Catua, a Tewa youth of Dry Spot (Tesuque)

Fernando de Cháves, a Spaniard who was near Red Willow (Taos) on August 10

Esteban Clemente, a Piro rebel leader who led a rebellion in 1664

Coronado, a Spaniard who explored New Mexico in 1539

Flat Nose, also known as Chato, a Tiwa revolutionary leader in Red Willow (Taos)

Alonso García, Lieutenant Governor of New Mexico in charge of the downriver area; also Captain General, second in command of the military

Francisco Gómez Robledo, a fifty-year-old Spanish military officer

Sebastián de Herrera, a Spaniard who, with his son, was near Red Willow (Taos) on August 10

Juan, a Tewa raised in Bead Water (Santa Fe)

Little Pot, known to the Spaniards as Francisco or Ollita, a Tewa of Water Gap (San Ildefonso)

Metal People, a name used for Spaniards by Tewas and others

Diego Misu, a fictitious inhabitant of Dry Spot (Tesuque)

Pedro Naranjo, a seventy-nine-year-old man, half-Black and half-Tlascalan Indian from Mexico, who lived at Rose Trail (Santa Clara) and aided the revolutionary Indians

Nicolás, the Spanish name of a Tewa man of Dry Spot (Tesuque)

Obi, a Tewa man of Dry Spot (Tesuque)

Omtua, a Tewa youth of Dry Spot (Tesuque)

Antonio de Otermín, Spanish Governor of New Mexico beginning in 1679

Francisco Pacheco, tuyo of Red Willow (Taos)

Popé, whose name means Ripe Squash, a middle-aged Tewa medicine man from Grinding Stone (San Juan); the most important revolutionary leader

Po-Se-Ye-Mo, the Tewa name for Rising Mist, a deity known under several similar names to nearly all village dwelling Indians along the Rio Grande

Saca, a Tiwa revolutionary leader from Red Willow (Taos)

Pedro Situ, a fictitious inhabitant of Dry Spot (Tesuque)

Tacu, a Tewa revolutionary leader of Grinding Stone (San Juan)

Tupatú, a Tiwa man of Mountain Gap (Picurís)

White Corn Maiden (or White Corn Woman), the supernatural being who Tewas believe is mother of the Winter People

Francisco Xavier, Secretary of Government and War in the Spanish government of New Mexico

Introduction

Almost one hundred years before the birth of the American Dream, a people rose up in bloody rebellion against the rule of the forces of the King of Spain in the valley of the Rio Grande in New Mexico. They rebelled because their own dream was in danger of fading away countless centuries after it had begun to unfold in the high canyon and mesa country of what is now the Southwestern United States. These were my people, the Pueblo Indians, and theirs was the first American revolution.

This revolution was fought for precisely the same reasons that the revolution of 1776 was fought—to regain freedom from tyranny, persecution, and unjust taxation. Only this native revolution was fought in 1680, ninety-six years before there was an America. It was a fight for freedom that has never been widely recognized as such, nor accorded the attention by historians that it might have had, had it been fought between Indians and Englishmen. But it is part and parcel of our common heritage as Americans, and it must be made part of our common consciousness. Our continued failure to recognize the Pueblo revolution is to ignore an important chapter in our common history along the way to nationhood.

During the first three-quarters of the seventeenth century, life for the Pueblo people was worse than life for the settlers of the original English colonies. The *encomienda* system, which was in effect in New Mexico between 1600 and 1680, provided for the involuntary seizure of a percentage of each Pueblo farmer's crop every year to support Spanish missionary, military, and civil institutions. It was similar to the system of tithing so familiar in the English-speaking world, only the amount taken was usually more than ten percent of each Pueblo farmer's yield. The *encomienda* system was especially burdensome because the Pueblo people had already been accustomed, perhaps for centuries, to contributing voluntarily a portion of their agricultural yield to a common storehouse for use by their own poor and their native religious leaders. With the coming of the Spaniards, then, the Pueblo people found themselves having to pay two taxes, one voluntary, the other not.

The institution of *repartimiento,* in turn, provided for forced Indian labor to work in Spanish fields. Other Indians were confined to sweatshops in the Governor's Palace in Santa Fe, weaving cloth, often without pay, for the Spaniards. For many years those who protested these and other abuses were punished by having their hair sheared.

And then there was the Inquisition, which spanned the seventeenth century, and often supplemented *repartimiento* by condemning other Indians to labor in the fields, sweatshops, or mines, usually on trumped-up charges of heresy and witchcraft. Also during the terrible decades of the Inquisition, the Pueblo people were persecuted for practicing their own religion, one which they clung to tenaciously because it had evolved through untold centuries of living in partnership with the land; and it had sustained them well through all this time. If ever there were ingredients to foment a righteous rebellion, it was in seventeenth-century New Mexico.

But these justifiable ingredients have long been

ignored. It took a man like Franklin Folsom to at last penetrate behind the regressive and culturally hidebound connotations of such phrases as the "Pueblo Indian Revolt" to demonstrate that there truly were two sides to those events in 1680. He demonstrates, further, that the Pueblo Indians were not merely engaged in a savage revolt against the enlightened and civilizing influences of Spanish civil and ecclesiastical powers, but were fighting for their right to live as a free people in dignity and peace.

Mr. Folsom's book has a still more profound significance for the Pueblo people. Because the events of 1680 took place so long ago and because subsequent histories have been based upon the uncritical use of flimsy, one-sided documents, the leaders of this just, noble, and successful uprising have been ignored whenever the roll of great chieftains has been called. Today even Pueblo Indians do not sing the praises of Popé, Saca, and Tupatú when posters of various chiefs are put up in college dormitories, when legends are reaffirmed, and when old men whisper together of bygone heroes. Yet Popé and his collaborators have always belonged together with Tecumseh, Joseph, Cochise, Manuelito, Crazy Horse, and other great leaders of Native America.

Of Popé, the chief strategist of the revolution,

we know little save that he was a holy man and a great man. But this is enough. Mr. Folsom demonstrates persuasively that Popé was not only a brilliant military tactician, but that he must have been a very humane leader to his own people as well. The two are not incompatible, although historians often have used testimony taken during and after the revolution to besmirch Popé's motives and reputation. This testimony was always recorded by Spaniards and often taken from frightened, recaptured Indians who were eager to curry favor with the Spaniards. After the reconquest in 1692, testimony was taken from Indians who were resigned to the long-range failure of their revolution. Hence the circumstances surrounding these documents did not encourage a sober assessment either of Popé or of his vision. Because of this, Mr. Folsom based his research not only upon a thorough grounding in the documents themselves, but also upon a careful, sympathetic study of Pueblo culture. This is a unique combination.

It will be well for young Indian people in this and future generations to know that one effort of their people to regain freedom was thoroughly successful for a time; that the defeat of Custer at Little Big Horn was not the only bright spot in their people's continuing struggle for survival. It will be good for them to know as well that the Indian history of this land consists of much more than the terrible tragedies at Fallen Timbers, Sand Creek, and Wounded Knee. These tragedies, real as they were, have already drawn too much emphasis in history and in the popular media. Besides, they are not the stuff from which dignity and confidence in self can be engendered.

What finally emerges from Franklin Folsom's patient, skilled, and dedicated labors is the story of a successful revolution, a revolution of a gentle and generally peaceful people who were driven to the threshold of suffering before they rose up and fought to regain their liberty. For me personally, Mr. Folsom's account brings those events to life vividly in a way that no previous account has before. For the first time, I feel that someone is writing about my people, and I am sure that many other Pueblo readers will agree with me when they, too, have had the opportunity to study *Red Power on the Rio Grande*.

As we approach the bicentennial of the American Dream and all that it stands for, it would also be well if we, Indians and all, reaffirmed our commitment to this first American revolution, now approaching its tricentennial. It was fought for the same principles.

This is not a book which will rest easy on anyone's shelf, as indeed it should not.

Alfonso Ortiz

1/ Call to Revolution

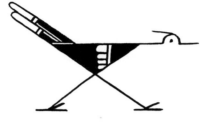

Roadrunner

Two young runners, their sandals in shreds, gasped out alarming news as they staggered into the small village of Dry Spot. Catua and Omtua, who were perhaps seventeen years old, had made a round trip of almost fifty-five miles since daybreak. They had started from Dry Spot and skirted around Bead Water, which was also called Santa Fe, nine miles to the south. From there they had trotted on to the place the Spaniards called San Cristóbal about eighteen miles to the southeast. It was here that the runners had picked up frightening information.

At daybreak, just before they jogged out of Dry

Spot, one of the War Chiefs had handed them a cord with knots tied in it. This cord was to go to the tuyo—Indian governor who had been appointed by Spaniards—at San Cristóbal. He would send it on relay-fashion to other villages.

Catua and Omtua knew very well that the cord was full of meaning. It bore a message about revolution. Indians were planning to regain the freedom they had lost to alien tyrants from Spain.

The War Chiefs had explained that the cord was going out only to men who were trusted because for years they had helped to plan the revolution. To show that they agreed with the message of the knotted cord, each leader who received it was to send up a smoke signal which would be seen over a great distance.

The tuyo of San Cristóbal did not send up a smoke signal when Catua and Omtua handed him the knotted cord. Instead, he leapt onto a horse he was privileged to own because he had been appointed to office by the Spaniards. Most Indians did not own horses. When they wanted to go someplace, they had to walk or run as Catua and Omtua had been doing since daybreak. The tuyo of San Cristóbal rode off toward the villages of Rising Leaf Lake and Turquoise Town.

This unexpected behavior troubled the young messengers. Instead of acting like a friend of the revolution, the tuyo acted like a friend of the Spanish governor Antonio de Otermín who lived in Bead Water and ruled over all the Indians of New Mexico for the far-off king of Spain.

As they watched him gallop off, Catua and Omtua wished more than ever that they had horses. With the help of these swift animals, they could rush their news to the War Chiefs in Dry Spot. But as luck would have it, there were not even any horses around to steal.

In order to report their strong suspicion that an Indian leader was betraying the revolution, Catua and Omtua had to tie on new yucca-leaf sandals and run back the whole long distance to Dry Spot. Skirting around Bead Water again, they dodged among juniper and piñon trees on the mountainside.

The two youths hoped they could run the twenty-seven miles on top of the twenty-seven they had already covered. They did more than hope—they knew they had to last out the distance. If they didn't, the whole revolution might fail simply because Otermín had found out the plans for it. The future of all Indians depended upon them. They had to warn the leaders in Dry Spot.

In front of the adobe buildings of the village they panted out their news to Obi and Nicolás, the first village leaders they met. These men were greatly disturbed and immediately sent the old town crier around the village to summon all the leaders to an emergency meeting.

Obi and Nicolás hurried to a secret place among the houses which the Spaniards had never discovered—a hole in the ground, easily covered by a stiff buffalo hide. The two men disappeared into the hole, climbing down a ladder to a sacred room called a kiva. Soon the other village leaders joined them.

Catua and Omtua, who were not old enough to attend such meetings, limped off to their separate homes and collapsed onto mats spread on the dirt floor. Almost at once they fell into sleep so deep that nothing disturbed them. They did not hear the sounds of mounting anger that came from the plaza as one man after another learned of the apparent treachery of the tuyo at San Cristóbal. They slept through the clatter of horses' hooves as Spaniards rode into the plaza. Orders yelled out in Spanish did not rouse them, nor did the rattle of swords and armor which had led the Indians to call all Spaniards the Metal People.

Catua and Omtua only woke when soldiers blustered into their homes. When each youth opened his eyes and saw a redheaded, middle-aged man in armor, looming over him, he knew that his worst fears had proved correct. The tuyo of San Cristóbal was a traitor who had got word to Otermín about the revolution. He had even told Otermín where his soldiers should look for the two messengers who had brought instructions for starting the movement for freedom. There was no other possible explanation for the presence of the officer Francisco Gómez Robledo, whom both of them recognized. None of the two-hundred village people would betray them—with the possible exception of one young fellow who had worked as a servant for Francisco Xavier, the official who was most diligent in trying to destroy Indian religion. All the other people in Dry Spot were friends. If any one of them should turn traitor, he would never be allowed to live here again. In fact, he would not be allowed to live.

Now as captives, Catua and Omtua were able to do what they could not do earlier in the day when they had been free. They rode—albeit with their hands in chains. And they were in Bead Water before sunset.

A gate opened as they approached the low, sprawling government buildings on the north side of the plaza. There, just inside the gate, the messengers of revolution saw a cannon. Soldiers, who were Spanish or half-Spanish, directed Indian slaves who had been brought from Mexico, as they wheeled the big weapon into a position from which it could fire on any local Indians who might gather in the plaza.

Inside the building, Governor Otermín, who had been in New Mexico only a short time, sat stiffly in a big chair behind a big table. Beside him at the table sat another Spaniard. This man held a feather which had been carved to a sharp point at one end. The young men from Dry Spot had seen medicine men brush sick people with feathers. They had seen prayer feathers offered to sacred spirits called Kachinas. They knew that feathers might have special meaning in wartime, but they had never seen a man use a feather to make marks on paper. This Spaniard made marks every time anyone spoke.

Behind the governor and secretary stood two armed guards, dark-skinned by comparison. Their mothers were Indians, Catua and Omtua assumed. Many children of mixed parentage worked for the Metal People. Many others were part of life in Indian villages.

A young Spaniard, whom Catua and Omtua recognized because he had grown up close to their home, began to give orders to them in Tewa, which was their language.

"Nicolás Catua and Pedro Omtua, you must now swear to God to tell the truth," said the young interpreter.

Catua and Omtua never used the Christian names which the Spaniards insisted on giving them. But it would serve no good purpose to object now, and they did as they were told. They swore they would tell the truth, and each touched a finger to his forehead, then to his breast, then to each shoulder, making the sign of the cross they had learned from the missionaries.

This formality over, Governor Otermín asked questions:

"Why are the Indians talking about attacking their friends the Spaniards?"

"Why would the Indians think of doing harm to their friends the holy priests?"

Catua and Omtua tried to look stupid.

At a nod from Otermín one guard unsheathed his sword. Another shook a big ox whip he held in his hand.

"Who are the leaders who are planning this treason?"

Both youths had an answer for this question: "We are too young to sit in council with the chiefs and with the leaders of the healing societies. We don't know what they say when they talk to each other."

"Who sent you out with messages to other villages?"

"Pedro Situ sent me," Catua said.

Omtua said that he had been sent by Diego Misu. Both young Indians hoped that Otermín would not discover that there were no such persons as Pedro Situ and Diego Misu.

"What is the meaning of the knotted cords you delivered to San Cristóbal?"

The messengers had replies ready. When the War Chief had handed the cords to them, he had told them what to say if soldiers of the Metal People captured them and threatened them with torture.

"These cords come from Po-Se-Ye-Mo," Catua answered. Even Governor Otermín would know that Po-Se-Ye-Mo was an important god who lived far to the north and was revered by all village Indians.

Otermín sniffed scornfully but listened as Omtua went on, talking as if he were very frightened.

"Po-Se-Ye-Mo has told all Indians to regain their freedom four days from now."

"Since this is August 9," said the secretary pedantically, "the Indians must be planning an uprising on August 13 in this Year of Our Lord, 1680."

Catua and Omtua had no idea why the War Chief asked them to give away this date for the revolution, but they knew the War Chief and trusted him. They did exactly as he had told them to do.

Now the youths, who spoke only the Tewa language, listened as Governor Otermín gave orders in Spanish. Guards, obeying, seized Catua and Omtua and pushed them outside to a spot on the covered walkway along the south side of the building which faced the plaza. In the plaza were Indians, including two friends they recognized from Dry Spot.

None of the Indians dared to greet Catua and Omtua. None called out words that would help them know whether or not the Indians still planned to go through with the revolution. As soldiers shoved them along, Catua and Omtua could not guess whether their capture meant the end of the Indians' hope for freedom.

Soldiers began to place firearms called harquebuses on gun rests and point them toward the crowd. Two men tied ropes around the boys' necks and tossed the free ends of the ropes up over roof beams that extended above the walkway.

Terror seized Catua and Omtua, and they tried to break away. But the guards had them well bound. Standing quietly, because they had to, Catua and Omtua looked into the stricken faces of their friends. In the dark eyes of the Indians, they saw no sign of anything the future might hold, except death.

Soldiers jerked on the ropes and hauled Catua and Omtua up off their feet. The boys did not hear the bitter cry that burst from the onlookers.

Several men in the crowd turned their backs on this latest of many executions in the plaza and raced toward Dry Spot bearing the tragic news.

At the same time, Governor Otermín began giving orders aimed at heading off the revolt which he had now heard from several sources was to begin on August 13. What Catua and Omtua had told him confirmed similar news he had already received from three widely separated villages.

Otermín had also heard another report, and this he simply could not believe. The Apaches, it was said, planned to rise up against the Spaniards in alliance with their old enemies the village-dwelling Indians.

However, Otermín sensed that something was definitely stirring. Fortunately, he thought, with four whole days ahead, he had time enough to prepare for trouble. By August 13, his defenses would be ready. Besides, the Indians were too stupid to think of any plan for rebellion that the Spaniards could not handle.

One step Otermín took without delay: He sent

a warning to the Spanish magistrate in each of the seven government districts in New Mexico. Those who carried these messages were men whom he trusted. To go to the village which Indians called Low Town but he called Galisteo, Otermín chose an Indian who as far as we know had no name except Juan and who had spent all his life among Spaniards. Juan spoke Spanish as well as he spoke Tewa. From the Indian governors of Low Town and other southern Tewa villages, and from what the priests had told him, Otermín judged that the southern Tewas would not rebel. They might in fact side with the Spaniards if war actually did break out. Juan rode off with a message of warning and an appeal for help.

Meanwhile, the men at Dry Spot moved with great speed. The moment that Catua and Omtua were arrested, the War Chiefs sent out new runners with new messages to every nearby village. From each of these villages fresh runners carried the message on still farther.

All these young men ran, hidden from the Metal People by darkness. The thin light of the old moon was gone, and the slender light of the new moon had not yet come. Any other men would have had almost to feel their way, but those chosen for this night knew the trails and made good speed. This time each runner carried a cord in which was only a single knot. The knot shouted to all who knew its meaning, "The revolution starts at dawn!"

In Dry Spot, Obi and Nicolás did not wait for the sun to rise. Following a custom understood among their people, they planned to start balancing the loss of Catua and Omtua by killing the first Spaniard they met. Tewa men could not permit the murder of any of their number to go unrevenged. The man they killed happened to be a young fellow no older than Catua and Omtua. He had not helped to arrest the runners nor had he helped to execute them, but that didn't matter. For the deaths of the runners, Spaniards had to die—and he was a Spaniard.

That night the inhabitants of Dry Spot prepared to kill more Spaniards. They prepared for war. Every man, woman, and child left the village, for the Metal People would surely attack. Well, let them attack and capture it. Dry Spot was only adobe mud; it could be rebuilt. It was the people of Dry Spot who really mattered. They must all be safe and free, and so they went to the mountains.

Up and down the valley runners delivered knotted cords, and from village after village columns of smoke rose in the early morning air on Saturday, August 10. These columns said as clearly as any written word, "We are rising and reclaiming our freedom."

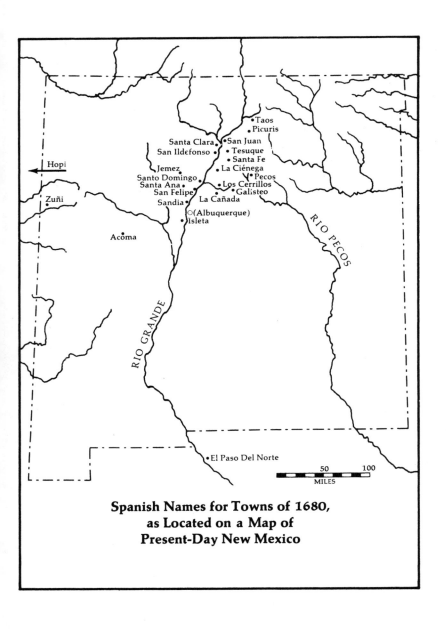

**Spanish Names for Towns of 1680,
as Located on a Map of
Present-Day New Mexico**

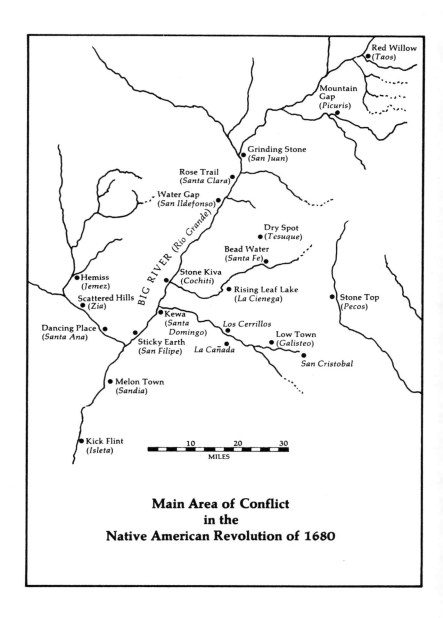

Red Willow
(Taos)

Mountain
Gap
(Picuris)

Grinding Stone
(San Juan)

Rose Trail
(Santa Clara)

Water Gap
(San Ildefonso)

Dry Spot
(Tesuque)

Bead Water
(Santa Fe)

BIG RIVER *(Rio Grande)*

Hemiss
(Jemez)

Stone Kiva
(Cochiti)

Rising Leaf Lake
(La Cienega)

Stone Top
(Pecos)

Scattered Hills
(Zia)

Kewa
*(Santa
Domingo)*

Los Cerrillos

Low Town
(Galisteo)

Dancing Place
(Santa Ana)

Sticky Earth
(San Filipe)

La Cañada

San Cristobal

Melon Town
(Sandia)

Kick Flint
(Isleta)

10   20   30
MILES

**Main Area of Conflict
in the
Native American Revolution of 1680**

2/ Aztlán Before 1680

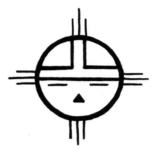

Sun God

It is hard today to know details about the desperate run that Catua and Omtua made. We have to guess how they felt when they discovered a traitor, endured a run nearly twice as long as a marathon, stood before the Spanish governor, and finally met death. The New Mexico Indians of the seventeenth century did not leave a single written record reporting what they did and why they did it. Spanish officials, on the other hand, left many such records. But these Spaniards were representatives of the powerful King Charles II, and they were mainly interested in trying to show that they had done no wrong and that the Indians had done no right. As a result, the events that surrounded the deaths of Catua and Omtua cannot be understood from existing documents—unless those documents are read upside down, as it were. They must be interpreted from the Indian point of view.

To understand why Catua and Omtua risked their lives—and lost them—it helps to look at a few earlier events along the watercourse that Indians called Big River and that Spaniards called the Rio Grande del Norte or simply the Rio Grande.

For more than ten thousand years, people have lived in and near the valley of the Rio Grande which flows from high peaks in southern Colorado through New Mexico and on along the border of Texas to the Gulf of Mexico. Today many people who have some Indian ancestry call this region part of Aztlán. According to legend Aztlán was the original home of the Aztec Indians, far north of the place in Mexico where they built their great nation.

At first the people of the river valley lived by hunting and by gathering wild seeds and roots and nuts. Then, perhaps four thousand years ago, travelers, who were probably traders, came from Mexico bringing some strange seeds that grew into plants that produced great quantities of new seeds if they were properly cared for. These plants we know as maize or corn.

Corn brought a great change in the lives of many men and women who lived in the region we shall call Aztlán. After they got corn seeds— and also the seeds of squash and beans—they planted small garden plots. Later they cultivated good-sized fields. Corn, squash, and beans became the main sources of food for an expanding population, and in time the people who grew these staples came to call them "the Three Sisters given us by Mother Earth."

To tend their gardens, the former wanderers had to stay in one place. Villages appeared. Men spent most of their time farming now, instead of hunting. Women who had been gatherers of wild seeds now became grinders of seeds that came from gardens.

Both men and women belonged to organizations and took part in ceremonies, some of which had come from Mexico with the corn, some of which had been elaborated on the spot. Those who grew corn successfully, prayed and danced and sang in certain patterned ways that satisfied them. They repeated stories that were approved and enjoyed by everyone. Some tales explained how people came to live on earth. They came, so the storytellers said, from dwelling places by a lake which lay underground. These first people emerged on the surface of the earth through an opening which some called the Sipapu. When people died, they returned underground as spirits. With new babies coming into the world and old men and women leaving it, there was a kind of balance established between the underground spirit people and the aboveground living people.

There were balances of other kinds, too, in the world of these farmers. In many villages half of the inhabitants called themselves Winter People and half called themselves Summer People. The Winter People and their chiefs and experts in ceremonies ran the village from November to March. The chief of the Winter People was the most important official at this time. The Summer People were in charge from March to November, and their chief was then the central figure. Every person in every village had some part to play; everyone had some importance, even if it was small. And everyone, no matter what his position, tried to live in harmony with the seasons and the land. Ceremonies and the planting of seeds, ceremonies and the coming of rain, ceremonies and the ripening of corn usually came around year after year in a dependable way.

But there were upsets from time to time in the regular pattern of existence. Some of these occurred when foreign Indians from the north came and stole corn which they did not know how to grow. For the most part the raiders were wandering Apaches and Navahos, two tribes which were closely related. Occasionally others joined in the raiding. One result was that farmers moved away from areas which were raided. Often these refugees settled in the Rio Grande Valley. Theft of their crops made them migrate but did not make them give up farming. Raiding was merely a great nuisance.

The Indians who robbed the farmers were in the habit of taking food wherever they found it. They took deer or antelope or buffalo when they could. In the same spirit, they carried away food from the farming villages.

The nomads did not attack a village in order to rule it or for the joy of killing. Almost always enough farmers survived after a raid to keep their way of life going.

For the most part, people seem to have shrugged off the attacks. Groups of farmers did not feel driven to band together for protection. On the contrary, individual villages subdivided. Some of the people would move away—perhaps because of disagreements, perhaps in search of new farmland that was less crowded. When this happened, one language began to be two dialects.

In time, the two dialects became two languages. With this budding-off of villages and languages, and with the coming of people from afar, the Rio Grande Valley and the land adjoining it became a complex concentration of settlements and tongues.

In spite of the continued activities of raiders, the separate villages still did not find it necessary to join together in any permanent way for protection. No government united them. Each one ran its own affairs, and each had its own ways.

There were seven distinct languages, and many dialects of some of these languages, spoken in the seventy or eighty farming villages in 1680. In villages that shared a common language, people in any one village were likely to say that people in all the others "spoke a little to one side." And these differences in dialect tended to hold people apart. Four of the seven distinct languages, though mutually unintelligible, were members of one language family—the Tanoan. They were about as closely related to one another as are German and Dutch and Swedish and English. These languages were Tewa, Towa, Tiwa, and Piro. Three others were as distinct from each other as are Chinese and Latin and Swahili. These unrelated tongues were Zuni, Hopi, and Keresan.

In spite of great language differences, the farming peoples in the various villages had many experiences in common. Their methods of growing crops were much alike everywhere. The wild plants and animals among which they lived were much like those of today in the same area, except that the animals were much more abundant.

The farmers held in common many ways of building houses and conducting ceremonies. They shared many customs. They dressed more or less alike. They followed similar patterns when they danced out stories and prayers. And one thing they all shared was a desire to live on, undisturbed, conducting themselves in ways that seemed right and that did not interfere with others. They all treasured their freedom to be themselves.

Four and one-half centuries ago a new wave of looters came into the region that is now the state of New Mexico. These invaders were Spaniards, and they behaved differently from the earlier invaders who were Apaches. The Apaches had entered the Rio Grande Valley to steal food. The Spaniards came looking for more than that. They sought riches. And the Spaniards' desire for wealth had a curious result. It made the Apaches much more predatory than they had ever been in the past. This is how it happened:

The Spaniards hired the Apaches to seize captives from tribes that roamed outside the area of Spanish control. The captives were valuable because they could be sold as slaves in Mexico. In payment for their part in this slave trade the Apaches got Spanish guns, powder, ball, steel knives, and swords. Now they were able to make more efficient raids on the village Indians in Spanish-held territory. And in time the weapons enabled the Apaches to steal from the very Spaniards who had supplied the arms in the first place.

The Spaniards, for their part, took not only food from the villages but freedom, too. The first of the Spanish adventurers who explored Aztlán was Coronado, who came in 1539 with horses, which the village dwellers had never seen before. His soldiers wore armor made of steel or many layers of leather, and they carried swords and terrifying guns. The village dwellers (who came to be called Pueblo Indians because *pueblo* is the Spanish word for village) were armed only with stone weapons. So it was easy for Coronado to force them to feed him and his soldiers and their horses.

After Coronado more Spaniards came, seeking quick riches in gold and other precious metals. Then in 1598 soldiers and settlers arrived in search of wealth by the slower method of farming or trading in goods they could get the Indians to produce. They also forced Indians to pay taxes to the Spanish king, and it was only by their labor that the Indians could discharge this puzzling debt. Nor was labor the only thing the Spanish settlers took from the Indians. They took much land as well.

With the settlers came missionaries who demanded that the Indians give up something still more precious—their religion. Soldiers protected both the missionaries and the land-grabbers, some of whom brought wives. Other settlers seized wives or concubines from among the Indians.

Herds of horses and cattle and great flocks of sheep accompanied the invaders. Later huge creaking wagons lumbered north from Mexico bringing tools and weapons and gunpowder and chocolate and wine and wheat flour—and the belongings of still more settlers. Many were convicts, sentenced to live a certain number of years in New Mexico. But the Spanish population grew more from births than from immigration. By 1680, more than two thousand of the twenty-eight hundred Spaniards in New Mexico had been born there, but they were as Spanish as they could be in this place which was very far removed from the center of Spanish culture.

Few among the Spanish New Mexicans were full-time soldiers, but many of the farmers did military duty. For this they received no pay. Instead they received from colonial officials the right to certain land and the right to have Indians work the land. With such privileges, a kind of feudal society grew up. Spaniards were the lords and Indians, the serfs. Almost every village Indian in New Mexico had to do some work for some Spaniard without pay.

And always there were missionaries, members of the Franciscan order, determined that the Indians should give up the ceremonies that had satisfied them for centuries. Dressed in their dark brown robes, the missionaries went about diligently trying to replace Indian rituals with other rituals that were approved by the king in far-off Spain. By 1680, they had established forty churches, all built by Indian labor.

The response of the village dwellers was friendly when Europeans first appeared with their priests, who were experts in conducting ceremonies, although very different from the Indians' own experts, the medicine men. A large number of Indians willingly accepted the new religion. It was their general belief that the more religious ceremonies they conducted, the better off they were, and so they added Catholic rituals to the ones they already had. All religions were good. They were like feathers in the wing of a bird. Under a well-feathered wing there was protection. With this thought in mind, people added Catholic feathers to the sheltering wing of their own religion, and not for a moment did they expect that they would have to give up old feathers as a condition for getting new ones.

Trouble developed inevitably as Catholic priests preached the doctrine that only their own beliefs were true and all others were false and had to go. To the village farmers, this attitude seemed arrogant and threatening. It angered many of them, and the anger mounted as Spanish priests increased their efforts to force Indians to give up their own religious practices and by so doing to limit the religious resources available to them. In the most dreadful single effort to force Indians into submission, Spanish soldiers seized five hundred people in White Rock and from each cut off a foot.

Everywhere in Aztlán there was profound anger at such acts, but angry or not, the village dwellers were influenced by the new way of life the Spanish invaders had brought.

Between 1598 and 1680 the Spanish soldiers, officials, and farmers also changed. They gradually discovered how to survive in the valley.

They reared children and grandchildren. Some of their descendants were light skinned, pure Spanish in ancestry. Others were dark skinned —half Indian. Most of the offspring of Spanish fathers were raised as Christians, and as time passed, more and more Indians found they could avoid trouble—and sometimes get favors—if they performed the Christian ceremonies. At the end of eighty years of colonial rule, sixteen thousand of New Mexico's Indians had gone through the ritual of baptism and were counted by the Spaniards as Christians. Among them were many who tended gardens for the missionaries or who cooked and cleaned for them or for soldier-farmers. Others worked in special factorylike rooms in Bead Water, weaving cloth which Spaniards used or exchanged for other goods they wanted from Mexico. In the villages, the Spaniards appointed some of the Christian Indians to be governors—tuyos—and other officials of lesser rank.

Alongside the Spanish-appointed officials, the Indians quietly kept leaders of their own choice— chiefs and heads of healing societies and other organizations. As a rule, no one talked about these secret leaders. It was wiser not to.

In various ways, the Indians were being forced into a kind of slavery. Many had to work without pay for Spanish farmers or priests. They saw much of the food they grew taken by Spanish officials. Generally speaking, Indians could not hold their old ceremonies openly in the village plazas. For these reasons and others, they became very angry at their masters. More than once, in more than one place, quiet people broke out in violent resistance.

In 1630, in villages where Zunis lived, the people were so bitter against missionaries that they filled one of them with arrows as he knelt holding his crucifix. A few days later Zunis killed another priest and held a dance in which they acted out the completion of the dead man's life, so that his spirit would not come back to bother them. They also gave him—as they gave to all who died—a ceremony admitting him to membership in a spirit organization. Among the spirits, he would have a home and so would not wander around doing mischief.

About 1645 in the village of Hemiss, the people planned a revolt together with Navahos. They started to carry out their plan and killed a Spaniard. The Spanish officials retaliated by executing twenty-nine villagers, whipping others, and selling still others into slavery. Indians at the village of Red Willow also rebelled, and in 1650 several villages united briefly, hoping thus to rid themselves of Spaniards. They had a well-worked-out plan: The rebels would strike while all the Spaniards were in church attending Mass on Holy Thursday. First they would turn the horses loose so that no one could escape. Then they would attack while the Spaniards were trapped inside the churches. This effort failed and nine leaders of the movement were hanged. Many others were enslaved for ten years.

In 1661, the leader of all the Franciscans in New Mexico gave harsh new orders against the religion of native Americans. Spaniards destroyed every object they could find that Indians used in their rituals. The zealous Franciscan leader reported that he had burned 1600 Kachina masks which men wore in certain ceremonies. The fact that Spaniards found so many of these forbidden articles shows that Indians were stubbornly trying to keep their customs alive.

In 1664, people in the south—in the downriver region where the language was Piro—united under a leader named Esteban Clemente. They, like earlier revolutionaries, planned to attack the Spaniards on Holy Thursday when they would be together in church. But the Spaniards discovered the plan and hanged Esteban Clemente.

In one village where Piros, in alliance with Apaches, had killed several Spaniards, six Piros were hanged.

In 1670, a famine swept the land. In order to get any taste of meat, many Indians—and some Spaniards—had to cut up and boil hides and ox harnesses. There was very little corn to cook into mush or to bake into bread. A great many people died of hunger. After this year of starvation, came a year in which a terrible epidemic—it may have been anthrax—sickened both cattle and people.

Following these disasters, the long train of wagons which brought supplies from Mexico every three years was exceedingly welcome. Normally it took a supply train about six months to lumber over the fifteen hundred miles of very rough trail from Mexico City to the capital, Santa Fe. The oxen and mules that pulled the heavy wagons moved slowly. The loads were enormous. Often as many as sixteen animals had to be hitched to a single wagon. Once a supply train had reached Santa Fe, it stayed there for several months while the wagons filled up with loads of hides that Indians had tanned and with cloth they had woven and salt they had collected and wrapped carefully in corn husks. While the wagons waited, another commodity was also collected—slaves. Then the wagons started back to markets in Mexico City, the capital of the Spanish empire in America.

These supply trains were exceedingly important to the Spanish-speaking settlers along the Rio Grande. In a special way that the Spaniards did not know, the supply train of 1680 was also exceedingly important to the Indians.

3/ Crisis

Bear Tracks

"How can we endure life under these tyrants? We starve while they make our men work in their fields."

"They make our women cook their meals and have their babies."

"They force our men to weave cloth which they take for themselves."

Thousands of Indians made complaints like these, and they had others.

"The Metal People destroy our shrines," they said. "They call our sacred Kachinas filthy names and force us to worship at *their* shrines. We cannot dance as our ancestors have always danced."

Village Indians made this protest with a deep feeling of pain. Why could the Spaniards not understand that their dances had a beautiful meaning? Each rhythm and pattern was intended to show that they respected life and wished to take their proper place in the world. How could they worship a strange god whose priests scorned the things that they held most dear? How could they live with men who broke everything they believed was good and beautiful?

Inevitably the protests led to the final question: "Why should we tolerate these men who seize but do not nourish? Why should we let them rule over us?"

When they thought of the famine of 1670 and the epidemic of the following year, it seemed no wonder that such disasters should crowd in and be part of a vast disorganization of life. The intruders had upset everything when they came into the valley. Their big wagons had brought wealth, but not to the Indians. Their longhorned oxen could pull great loads, and they provided much meat. But the loads did not belong to Indians, and it was not Indians who feasted on beef.

The very god these invaders said everyone

must worship seemed a thing of pain. He was nailed to a cross, and sharp thorns bit into his head.

The pain-bringing invaders seemed angry at everything they found. They could not value the fruitful partnership in which Indians and land lived together. They could not respect the way corn and people depended each on the other, nor the way both prospered under the blue sky and grew, well nourished by rains and the water of the great river.

The invaders had not quietly entered the valley and modestly learned where there was room in it for more living. Instead, they seized the valley and acted as if it, and everyone who lived there, had a duty to serve their ends. To them, the valley was a weapon, not a companion. It was a dagger with which they set about carving out more of the kind of life they had lived—or had wanted to live—in a distant place called Spain.

The invaders could not cooperate with nature. They had to rule it. Often they could not even cooperate with each other. The brown-robed priests quarreled with the soldier-farmers, trying to gain control over the valley and the people who had always lived there, calm and at one with the place. Both priests and military men seized farming land and then made Indians cultivate it. Each of the farmer-soldiers wanted to be rich—richer than his neighbors. None of them cared about the Indians they sent to the fields except that they wanted these dark ones to work hard and quietly do as they were told. Often the Indians had to obey laws that had been decreed in Spain, on the other side of the world, before any Spaniard had ever seen Aztlán.

"How can we go on with life so torn apart?" the village Indians asked.

The Spanish governor in New Mexico heard some of the questions. So, too, did Brother Andrés Durán, missionary at Water Gap. In 1675, he urged the governor to stop the questions by closing the mouths of the more vocal of the Indian leaders. These leaders were not appointed by the Spaniards to be officials in the various villages. Rather they were men who seemed to the Indians to know beautiful, comforting ways of helping people to fit into a world in which rains usually came when the corn needed moisture. The wise men knew how to help others to respect themselves and to be respected. They knew intricate ceremonies and satisfying stories about the past. They helped people dance and sing out their feelings and take suitable names and fit into their special places in the web of life. They tried to help people return to health when something went wrong and upset the harmonious adjustment of the body as a part of all nature. Medicine men, these wise healers were called.

The Spanish governor in 1675 agreed with Brother Andrés that control of the restless, questioning, angry Indians would be easier if the medicine men were silenced. So he ordered soldiers to go out into the villages. There, possibly in dark rooms called kivas, used secretly as ceremonial chambers, the soldiers might find the sorcerers, as the governor called them. Wherever they were, they must be seized and brought to the capital to stand trial for practicing witchcraft and being generally in league with the Devil.

Aided in their search by certain of the Indians who were converts to Christianity and who felt that their future lay with the Spanish rulers, the soldiers found forty-seven medicine men.

Each time a medicine man was dragged before the judge, some farmer-soldier or Franciscan missionary or converted Indian accused him of an act of witchcraft or blasphemy or idolatry. To the medicine man, this same act had a profoundly religious meaning. Perhaps he had performed a dance wearing a mask. Perhaps he had uttered a prayer beside a small hole in a kiva floor, called the Sipapu to remind people of the opening from which their ancestors had emerged from the womblike underworld. Perhaps he had sprinkled cornmeal on the ground, making a trail for helpful spirits to follow—or setting up a barrier that would keep out spirits who wanted to work evil.

As each witness gave his evidence, the magistrate accepted this indication of non-Christian behavior as proof of illegal activity, and he pronounced sentence.

It was said of four of the medicine men that they tried to work a spell against a Christian priest. The sentence was death. Where all could see, in the big plaza in Bead Water, these four men—revered by Indians—were hanged. Also in the plaza where all could see, jailers whipped the other forty-three beloved leaders, then threw them into dungeons.

Word of this attack on their leaders and their religion spread quickly through all the villages, leaping language barriers. Christian converts shared the feeling of outrage. Soon a large number of Christians from the Tewa-speaking village of Grinding Stone walked in a body to the Spanish capital. The trip took all day, but the Christians lost none of their anger along the way.

The people from Grinding Stone had a very high regard for one of the imprisoned medicine men who came from their village. They called him Popé. No one had ever tried to do more for them than this trusted man. Somehow he made them want to live, and there had been many times when they were so miserable that they longed for death. This Popé had about him something of genius. He did not give orders and demand work. His way of leading was to think and to share his thoughts and to help people feel that they and he held good thoughts in common. In ways hard to put into words, Popé helped the people feel right about life.

4/ Popé

Kiva Steps

No one has recorded what Popé looked like. We don't know whether he was tall or short, fat or lean. Apparently there was nothing remarkable about his appearance. If he was like other village Indians of his time, he was short by modern standards—perhaps only about five feet four inches tall. He was probably modest in bearing. Most village-dwelling men were—and are. The communities along Big River have never encouraged star performers, braggarts, egotists. Certainly the meaning of Popé's name is modest. It was given to him in a ceremony of the kind held for all Tewa babies.

At the time of his birth, which may have been about 1630, two women attended his mother as midwives. After he was born, the mother and the baby stayed indoors for four days. During that time villagers came to call and to wish the best possible kind of life for the infant. Each visitor stood over him and made a gathering motion with both hands. This motion was meant to collect all sickness and bad luck. After gathering in all misfortune, each visitor made a motion as if throwing it far away to the west. At the end of three days the midwives chose an ear of corn that was filled out perfectly with white kernels and another ear that was filled out perfectly with blue kernels. They put aside a small broom and a pottery bowl and collected certain objects that were filled with the spirit of life because they had been used by living people in times past. After that, at dawn on the fourth day, one of the midwives carried the baby and the two ears of corn out of doors. These two ears stood for White Corn Woman and Blue Corn Woman, who, according to the Tewas, were the mothers of all their people. One midwife, using the little broom, swept the air over the baby with motions that said she was moving all good things toward the little one. Then the other midwife, who was called the Name Mother, held the baby and the ears of corn out in six directions—south, west, north, east, up, and down. At the same time she prayed and uttered the name she had chosen for the baby.

The name she chose was Ripe Squash. This seemed appropriate because the baby had been born in the season when squashes are ready to harvest. In the Tewa language, the word for Ripe Squash is *po-pé*. And Popé is the name by which Ripe Squash has become more widely known than any other man from the farming villages of his time or of any time.

Popé grew up in Grinding Stone. Before he was a year old, important leaders held a ceremony for him and all other young babies. As part of the ceremony, two assistants to the chief of the Summer People held wooden objects that resembled folding carpenter's rules. At a certain point, they opened these folded sticks as a way of saying that they hoped the world would open out far ahead of the young Popé. The men with these folding "World Stretchers," acted for the whole village and wished Popé a long life. Another way of wishing the best for the child was to give him a drink of sacred water from an abalone shell that had been brought by traders all the way from the Pacific Coast. And for his benefit, and the benefit of all the other children his age, an altar was erected. On it stood a rainbow made of wood. The colors in the rainbow were black and green and yellow—the colors sacred to the Summer People. Black stood for the dark clouds that produced precious rain. Green was for growing crops, yellow for life-giving sunshine.

For the next five or six years Popé played around the village and watched and enjoyed and learned. He watched the older boys playing a game with sticks and a leather ball, and when he was big enough, he played too. He listened when the old town crier called out, in the four different plazas, his news that someone had lost a necklace or a stone knife. The old man also reminded people when it was time for them to sweep the streets and paths, and when it was time for them to go out and repair the irrigation ditches—or best of all, when it was time to get ready for footraces.

Popé learned many things as he grew up. He listened as older people told him: "We Tewas eat gently. We recognize that a plant that was once growing is now going to be part of our lives."

Popé learned the directions and the colors that always went with them. Old men told Popé and other children long and fascinating stories about how their people had come up from an underground place called Sand Lake and finally reached Grinding Stone. Along the way they found many animals and plants that were useful to them, and Popé began to learn about these. Deer and elk and bear and bighorn sheep and wild turkeys all roamed near Grinding Stone.

Popé learned that radiating out from a central spot in the village were many places of special importance. Very near the town were four sacred shrines. One was called Sun-Water-Wind. Another was named after an important deity called Spider Woman. A third was for a god—Ash Youth. The fourth was called Large Marked Shield.

Four flattopped hills beyond the shrines were the homes of special spirits. And beyond these hills—far beyond—rose the very sacred peaks: Shimmering Mountain, Obsidian Mountain, Turtle Mountain, and Stone Man Mountain. Someday Popé would go, as grown men did, to say prayers on all these peaks which lifted men to the sky.

When Popé was about seven, the grown-ups in the village held another ceremony for him and all the children his age. The adults—even those who were Winter People—paid a lot of attention to the Summer People's children. The Winter People came to the special dance held at this time.

They said they came to "seek life" for the children.

With each ceremony, Popé entered more deeply into the life of the village. When he was ten, he was part of a ceremony in which he was said to be "finished." He now had the right to act out the part of gods in some of the ceremonies. He could wear the mask that represented a god and behave the way that god was supposed to. From now on he could take part in the religious life of his village. The ceremony served the same purpose as the confirmation ceremony of the Christians in Grinding Stone. When Indians were confirmed by priests, they were supposed to be full members of the Catholic Church. But Popé noticed that no Indian ever became a priest. Only Spaniards held that important post in the church, but any Indian boy who worked hard and learned the countless things he had to know could become a leader in a medicine society.

One part of the ceremony which admitted Popé to full membership in the village was designed to help him—and the whole village—by driving any evil out of him. Men in masks who were called Kachinas and who represented supernatural beings, whipped him to drive out the evil. This whipping was not punishment for bad things Popé had done. It was not like the whippings ordered by missionaries when Indians failed to attend Mass. It was rather a way of protecting him from evil spirits that might get into him and do harm. And when the whipping was over, the Kachinas took off their masks, and Popé saw that each Kachina was also a man—a man whom he knew—a neighbor who was acting the part of a supernatural being. Popé's experience may have been a little like the experience people have today when they go to a play. During a play an actor is the character he impersonates. Then when the play is over, and the actor steps out on the stage and bows to the audience, he is a different person altogether.

As Popé grew up, he had many things to learn. One thing was that four was a magic number. In addition to the four sacred mountains, four sacred hills, and four sacred shrines outside Grinding Stone, there were four plazas inside the village. Dances were performed four times, once in each of the plazas. In some of the dances, the performers turned facing for a moment in each of four directions. In a way, four meant good luck, just as among Spaniards it was often supposed to be a good idea to say something three times. In a ceremony he performed as he crossed into

New Mexico, the conqueror who seized the area
announced that he took possession "once, twice,
and thrice" in the name of the Spanish king.

Sometimes when the Spaniards weren't watch-
ing, the War Chief called out the Kossas. A
Kossa made all kinds of jokes and played tricks
on people and teased those who did silly things.
He, as well as the serious Kachinas, was a part of
village religious life. Spaniards could easily recognize a Kossa because he wore two horns on his
head and had broad horizontal stripes painted
on his body. If they saw a Kossa, they would
burn his headdress and punish him. They also
burned Kachina masks whenever they found
them. People in Grinding Stone had to be very
careful to choose the right times for Kossas or
masked figures to appear.

They had to be careful about many things.
They had to pretend that the parrots and eagles
they kept in cages were only pets. Actually the
birds were sacred, kept because they produced
feathers that were important in ceremonies.

When Popé had been "finished," he was allowed to enter Little Kiva, which was a religious
room belonging to the Summer People—or rather
to the men among the Summer People. The
women usually could not enter. They were said
to have special powers which could cause bad

luck when men hunted or waged war or conducted ceremonies. To protect these and other activities from the mysterious dangers that came from women, men had special organizations and meeting places for themselves.

As Popé learned more of the life around him, he became interested in the work of the healing societies. There were two in Grinding Stone. One was the Flint Society, the other was the Fire Society. The leaders of these societies conducted ceremonies before footraces. They blessed the fields before planting in the hope that evil influences would not hurt the crops and hence do harm to the people. Leaders of the medicine societies also spent much time doing what they could to cleanse people of sickness.

Being a leader of a medicine society was a very complicated job—probably the most difficult one in the village. Popé decided to take all the training that was necessary to become a medicine man. The training lasted for years and required a good memory and great perseverance. Popé had to learn perfectly a great number of different rituals and songs and dances. He had to know all the legends that his people accepted as explaining life. He had to know the meaning of countless symbols on masks, on altars, on prayer sticks, on costumes.

An Indian religious leader was as learned in his way as a Christian missionary in his. And an Indian ritual expert was very important to the people among whom he lived. He gave form and meaning to their lives. Perhaps the most important thing Popé learned as he went through his long training was this: What a Tewa thinks inside himself and what he does in the outside world should never contradict each other. They should be the same.

All this meant that Popé was heading for a collision with the Spaniards. So, too, was every other medicine man. The Spanish officials were trying to stamp out every vestige of native religion. From the moment Popé began his training for leadership in a medicine society, he became an outlaw in the eyes of the Spanish rulers. He remained an outlaw throughout his adult years. During those years, he devoted himself to trying to help his people and to protecting their way of life from destruction.

Often he withdrew into a dark room. The Spanish soldiers and priests thought that this simple chamber was just a storeroom and so they never bothered it. However, the room was really a private retreat for prayer. There Popé could reflect, undisturbed, on the plight of his people.

And he could think of ways to help them out of their slavery.

Often as an aid to his reflections, Popé took cornmeal from a special pouch and, pinching it between his thumb and forefinger, deftly sent a thin trickle of the white powder onto the floor of the kiva. The line he traced with cornmeal stretched farther and farther along the dark floor. To it, he added lines of gray sand and black charcoal, powdered fine. A design took shape— a design made up of many symbols, each one full of meaning for those who saw it. Put together, the symbols reminded people of age-old stories; and the stories, people felt, expressed their wishes. Near this dry painting was another symbol, the Sipapu.

In the meditation room, Popé sometimes built an altar with special little wooden slats, colored in many ways, reflecting rain and life and hope. Before the altar he placed prayer sticks. These, too, were symbols. Popé kept the sticks in a special basket. He kept other symbols in a pouch carefully made from the skin of a bear's leg. A bear was sacred and had special meaning to the village dwellers along Big River. It seemed more like a brother, more human than any other animal they knew.

All around Popé were symbols that could be seen or touched, and they served him just as symbols printed on pages served people who read their prayers.

After performing a ritual, Popé sometimes reported an idea or a dream he had. It seemed to him that gods said it would help Indians if they all united. They should stand together against those who were trying to take from them their identity as Indians. Many times Popé helped people to feel that Po-Se-Ye-Mo—Rising Mist—the god who linked the sun and the earth, wanted Indians to be themselves, not just something useful to strange men who had harsh aims in life.

5/ Popé Becomes a Leader

Bear

In his ceremonies, Popé sometimes put the paw of a brown bear, glove-fashion, over his right hand. It was as natural for him to wear this brown paw as for a Franciscan missionary to wear a brown robe. Both the paw and the robe were outward symbols of certain inward beliefs.

Because Popé, when he wore his bear paw, was a trusted healer, and because all his beliefs and all his actions made a harmonious whole, people listened when he spoke. They listened with aching, desperate attention when he found many ways of saying, "Indians must once again be Indians."

While Popé and other medicine men prayed and performed their rituals, the Spaniards were not idle. For one thing there was the arrest in 1675 of the forty-seven medicine men accused of witchcraft. Both the Spaniards and the Indians in seventeenth-century New Mexico believed that there were such things as witches. The Indians looked for these evildoers among their own people. The Spaniards, on the other hand, often sought them outside their own community —among the conquered Indians. One Spanish punishment for witchcraft was whipping.

When Popé was publicly whipped by the Spaniards in 1675—and then thrown into a dungeon—his fellow townsmen demanded his freedom. Indeed they demanded the freedom of all the arrested medicine men. The Tewas from Grinding Stone told the Spanish governor as a simple fact that either one of two things would happen if the medicine men were not freed.

One possibility, dreadful for the Spaniards to consider, was that every Indian in the valley would move away. This would leave the Spanish officials, landowners, and missionaries with no one to do the work they liked to have done for them. If the Spaniards did not want to starve, they would have to produce their own food.

The other possibility, even more dreadful, was

that the Indians would decide to stay in the valley and would drive the Spaniards away. In all New Mexico there were fewer than 150 Spaniards trained and equipped to be soldiers in time of emergency. Of these, only thirty-five were real soldiers. Moreover, for every Spaniard there were ten village Indians, and if these Indians really decided to drive the Spaniards out, there could be terrible trouble.

In the face of such alternatives, the governor who had ordered the arrest of the medicine men thought it would be too risky to keep them in prison, so he set them free.

Popé, weakened by his whipping and imprisonment, but strengthened by new hatred, walked back to Grinding Stone. There he resumed the very activities for which he had been arrested. He went into a kiva and made dry paintings, tracing out designs with black and green and yellow lines as he had always done. He tried to figure out what Po-Se-Ye-Mo, the one who scattered mist, would advise his people to do.

What Popé had to say when men visited him in the kiva must have been something like this:

"The Metal People have taken our best fields, then made us plant corn for them to eat. The priests of the god of the Metal People make us tend their sheep. We shear wool from the animals, then weave wool into blankets which wagons carry away to the south. These same priests burn our masks, then hold up their cross for us to worship. All this will go on and on until with one voice we say, 'No more!' If all of us in the Tewa villages say, 'No more!' the Metal People will be frightened. If all of us in all villages say, 'No more!' the Metal people will have to set us free.

"We must forget the ways in which each village differs from all the others. We must remember the ways in which we are alike—and suffer alike. We must agree that none of us, even in the villages of the Tiwas or of the far-off Big Leggings, should be slaves. We should not have to take Spanish names or imitate the customs of our conquerors, hoping thus to be allowed to stay alive.

"Beyond the Tewa people, we must unite with the Keres people and the Towas of Hemiss and Stone Top. All of us have lost our freedom. Together, but only together, we can win it back."

This was strange talk in Grinding Stone. The village had never joined with other villages in an alliance. Even against the attacks of the Apaches, Grinding Stone had fought its own battles. Popé's new idea took some thinking about.

With reminders that Tewas and all village dwellers would get strength from their old rituals, Popé began in every way possible to encourage people and to organize them—a task that would take several years. Traders who traveled from one village to another now carried ideas of unity as well as packs that contained turquoise or dyes or feathers or seashells or pots. Each trader spoke more than one language. Some knew several. With their knowledge of the various tongues spoken in the villages, the traders— month after month, year after year—helped the idea of revolution to leap the many language barriers.

Medicine men, too, traveled to take part in ceremonies away from home or just to visit. They also knew more than one language, and they helped spread ideas throughout the area, which stretched 150 miles from north to south and twice that far from east to west.

Working through both traders and medicine men, Popé helped people to cling to their own beliefs and at the same time to accept the new idea that all Indians should work together. In most villages, at least one leader appeared who saw the importance of Popé's plan for unity. In Grinding Stone there was such a leader. His name was Tacu. Men from everywhere began to find reason to visit Grinding Stone and there to join Tacu and Popé.

In Red Willow, the most northerly of the villages, a medicine man named Saca had been drawn to Popé's ideas. Saca began to urge his people, who spoke Tiwa, to forget their old distrust of Tewas. Flat Nose, another leader, did the same.

In Kewa a man named Catiti joined in the work of preparing people to take back their freedom. In the Tiwa-speaking village of Mountain Gap, a man named Tupatú became the revolutionary leader. And so it went from village to village. In almost every place where village Indians lived, they began to talk about working together for the right to be themselves.

Spanish officials in Grinding Stone grew uneasy as they sensed the spread of the spirit of defiance among the people there. Perhaps the Spaniards had information about the actual plans for unity that were coming out of the kiva where Popé went for meditation. There was indeed a way in which some news might have reached the Spaniards. Popé's daughter may have heard some of the things her father was saying, and she may have repeated some of what she had heard to her husband, Nicolás Bua. Bua, as it happened, was the Indian whom the Spaniards had appointed to act as tuyo of Grinding Stone. Because he got his authority from the Spaniards, he might have thought it to his advantage to tell them about the developing plans for revolt.

Popé suspected Bua of being a traitor. According to one report, Popé himself, in his own home, executed Bua. According to another account, certain men of Grinding Stone killed him in a field outside the town. Whatever it was that happened to Bua, Popé definitely resolved to limit knowledge of the plans for revolution to as few persons as possible. He remembered well the disaster that had befallen the Piro-speaking villages far downriver a few years before when someone betrayed to the Spaniards their plans for an uprising, and well-loved Piro leaders had been hanged. The terror which descended on the Piros was great, and many of them had been profoundly frightened. People so frightened—and so far away—had better not be trusted with the secrets of the new revolution. And so the Piro villages were left out of Popé's plans.

Much of the danger of a leak would disappear if most people in the villages did not know the plans. Children under the age of fifteen probably did not know of the plans, and half the adult population certainly didn't need to know any plans because it would not be engaged in fighting. That was the female half. It so happened that many Indians feared women could have a bad effect on war-making. Women had never been included in war councils. They, like Spanish women—like women almost everywhere then and now—were given lesser roles to play by the men who wielded power. So, making use of old beliefs, Popé urged that all secret plans be kept from them.

In spite of every precaution that Popé took, however, disturbing rumors continued to reach the Spaniards, and the Spanish officials continued to suspect the medicine man at Grinding Stone. Francisco Xavier, Secretary of War for all New Mexico, and a most zealous hater of native American religion, warned Popé to cease his agitation or be punished.

Popé saw that if he was to be free to organize he would have to leave his village, and this he did. He went to Red Willow. There he was welcomed by Saca. Nearby in the village of Mountain Gap, Tupatú was also very glad to see him.

Not only did Popé have able lieutenants in these men, but in Red Willow he was much more free to work for revolution than he had been in Grinding Stone. There were no relatives around him advising him to be cautious—for their sakes. None of the rules that applied in Grinding Stone limited him here where he was a foreigner and hence was expected to be different. He could speak now as freely as he pleased. He could say and do things that Red Willow men did not always feel free to say and do. So with his move from Grinding Stone to Red Willow, Popé's work for revolution picked up speed.

The people of Aztlán had often seen Spanish weapons. A few of the Indians on the sly had even learned to use them. They knew how to load the heavy harquebuses that the Spanish soldiers carried. But the Indians had no harquebuses of their own. If they were to get these weapons, they would have to capture them. So, too, with horses. All the Spaniards had horses, but very few Indians owned any. However, many Indians had learned how to ride, and they knew that if they could get mounts, they would be able to face the mounted Spanish soldiers on much more equal terms than if they had to fight on foot. Arrows were poor weapons against the steel armor that some Spaniards wore or the leather armor with which others protected themselves. But not every inch of a Spaniard could be covered by steel or leather. Arrows or spears could find openings. Nor did every Spaniard own armor.

Each Indian village had a society for conducting relations with other villages or other tribes. Because one function of the society was to protect a village from attack, it was called a War Society and its leader was a War Chief. The members of these societies did not spend a great deal of time practicing the arts of war, but they did fight on occasion—for example, when Apaches attacked, seeking corn. The members of the War Society were not highly trained professional soldiers; they were content to protect their homes.

Popé realized that the revolution would be strengthened if it had on its side warriors who were more like professional soldiers. The Apaches were famous fighters. Popé urged that the village dwellers try to get these ancient enemies to become their allies. When people heard this idea, they were astonished at first; but the more they thought about it, the more sense it seemed to make. Everybody could see that the Apaches, like the Pueblos, hated the Spaniards, and with good reason. Spanish soldiers and farmers often seized Apache children and enslaved them. To the Spaniards an Apache child had market value. A boy or a girl could be traded for a good mule.

It didn't matter that the Apaches were paid by

the Spaniards for bringing in the children of
Plains Indians to be slaves. The Apaches treasured their own children as much as any people
do, and they often raided Spanish farms hoping
to recover boys or girls who had been taken from
them. The Apaches always took whatever else
of value they could carry away. In this way they
added to their arsenal of sharp Spanish knives
and deadly Spanish guns. The Pueblos looked at
the Apaches' arms and saw how good it would
be to have them used against the Spaniards.

"We will be stronger with the Apaches at our
side than we would be with them at our back,"
Popé reasoned, and people came to see the sense
of this.

Gradually a plan for freedom—a plan for revolution—took shape. Catiti, Saca, Flat Nose,
Tupatú, Little Pot, and others besides Popé con-
tributed to developing the strategy and tactics of
the action they felt they must take. Wherever
possible they would seize Spanish horses and
weapons to use against the tyrants.

In making their plan, they came to think of
Spanish colonial power as a long snake stretch-
ing up Big River with its head in the north.

"Cut off the head, and you kill the whole
snake," was Popé's theory. The head was the
capital at Bead Water. If the Indians could sepa-

rate the capital from the outlying Spanish settlements and farms, the Spaniards everywhere would be weakened, without leadership. Without the capital to rely on, they would find it hard to work together against attack.

Another part of the plan went this way: "Send word to the downriver settlements that the capital has fallen. Send word upriver that all downriver is under our control." Rumors like this would confuse the Spaniards, weaken their confidence, and make them easier to defeat. Patrols and guards along the trails and roads would keep Spaniards from getting reliable information or sending for help or escaping.

With attention to every detail, Popé and the other leaders worked out plans. Among the leaders were men who knew the Spaniards well.

6/ Choosing the Time

Water Serpent

"When should we strike?" This question came up again and again.

It would obviously make good sense to strike when the Metal People were weakest. But when would that be? How could the Indians tell?

It would be best to attack when the Metal People had used up most of their powder and when their old firearms were worn-out. The village dwellers must strike for freedom when Spanish storerooms were empty.

Popé knew that the Spaniards were hungriest for everything just before the arrival of the supply train which came from Mexico every third spring or summer. This was the year when the great caravan was due.

The Metal People would be waiting for new harquebuses and more powder and ball to use in them. The wagons would bring new swords, daggers, and shields. There would also be more armor and more horses—horses that could trample the Indians underfoot.

Of special importance was one other fact that Popé knew: This year the supply train would be late.

Popé, like all Tewas, had watched the weather carefully all his life. Now he was studying it with the greatest possible attention, and what he observed had dramatic possibilities for the revolution.

The snowfall in the mountains above Big River had been heavy in the winter of 1679-1680. The spring that followed was cool, so the snow was late in melting. When the hot days of July did arrive, the melting was sudden and massive. The waters of Big River rose and rose. Where the river was usually shallow enough for fording, the water was deep and swift, and it flooded outward over low banks making it impossible for wagons to cross.

If the supply train reached Big River in July, it would be stopped on the far side by the unusually high water. Popé knew this and so did other leaders. As long as the wagon train was motionless on the far side, the munitions that were so vital to the Spaniards would be held up. They would be useless. And if the midsummer rains came soon enough to keep the water high, the supply train would have to wait still longer.

Popé, Catiti, Saca, Flat Nose, and others watched the weather. They watched the level of water in the river, and finally they decided that the supply train would be held up, far to the south, until late in August. Obviously the best time for the rising would be earlier in August— about the time when the first corn was getting ripe. This would be in the second week of August on the Spanish calendar.

Messengers went out all over Aztlán with the news that definite plans for the rising had now been made and that the date had been set and would be announced later. It was important that each messenger should explain the plan correctly. So Popé and his colleagues used a device that people in Red Willow had learned from Indians who lived on the Great Plains and who occasionally came to visit them. They painted pictures on deer hides, which the messengers carried with them. Each picture was a private symbol to remind a messenger of certain things he was to say.

If he was captured by Spanish soldiers, he could tell anything he wanted to about the pictures—except the truth.

The deerskins on which the revolutionary leaders painted their symbols have been lost. Today we don't know what those symbols were, but the messengers knew and understood them. The painted hides went from village to village as far west as the distant home of the Big Leggings people, and the most responsible men in Aztlán knew that the time for revolution was at hand.

No one dreamed that the tyrants could ever be persuaded to leave the country merely because it was right and just for them to depart. Only force could free this land which had been seized by force and held by force. If the Spaniards could be induced to leave peacefully, that would suit the Indians very well. It would not then be necessary to kill any of them and to risk Indian lives in the process. None of the leaders, however, had any doubt that some of the enemy must be killed in order to persuade the others to leave. And the killing had to be carefully planned if it was to do its grim work of persuading.

"Upriver, outside Bead Water, every single Metal Person must die—all of them. There can be no exceptions. Governor Otermín must be convinced that we will kill all the Metal People in Aztlán if they don't leave." This was the way Popé reasoned. This was the way all the rebel leaders reasoned . They agreed that upriver every man, woman, and child must be killed in the first hours of the revolution. The attacks must all be made at the same time. Clearly, if the Indians struck everywhere at once, the Metal People would not be able to help one another. There were not enough soldiers in Bead Water to defend all the farms and estates and settlements and churches at the same time.

As soon as the revolutionaries destroyed the Metal People upriver, they planned to give Governor Otermín and his followers a chance to leave Aztlán. If Otermín wouldn't leave peacefully, they would drive him out or destroy him.

The leaders of the revolution shared this idea, and they told it to trusted men in much of the valley.

The corn began to grow ripe, and the season for the rising drew near, but the Indians had no calendars. They had to work out some other device so that the rising would take place everywhere on the same day at the same hour.

Someone, perhaps it was Popé, came up with the idea of sending out runners with knotted cords. The number of knots would indicate the number of days left before the rising was to begin at dawn.

Many leaders in upriver villages knew the general plan. But Popé, Catiti, Saca, and a very few others shared the secret part of it with no one. Remembering his son-in-law, Popé was not sure that any tuyos could be trusted even though they seemed to support the revolution. At the last moment some of them might think that their future was safer with the Spaniards from whom they got their power and privileges. They might betray the revolution and give Otermín the warning he needed in order to defeat the great plan.

How, then, could these undependable men be handled?

It must have been Popé who suggested sending out a false date for the rising. If Otermín heard of this date, he would begin to make preparations with the wrong date in mind. And if Otermín's soldiers got busy all of a sudden, the revolutionaries would know that they had been betrayed. If they watched to see who ran to Otermín, they would know who the traitors were. This false date must be later than the real one. Thus Otermín would think he had more time to make his plans than he really had. Then the Indians could move against him before he was ready. In addition, this scheme would have the traitors working for the revolutionaries instead of doing them harm.

The handful of leaders who heard these proposals approved. A brilliant plan was now ready to be put into effect—a plan that had many ingenious parts, each carefully fitted into all the others:

First, the multi-lingual traders would overcome the language barriers and prepare the way for revolution while appearing to do business as usual.

Later, runners with painted deerskins and knotted cords would carry wordless messages which all leaders could understand.

When the moment for action came, warriors without modern weapons were to seize such weapons from the enemy.

By falling upon small scattered settlements first, the rebels would risk least damage to themselves.

At the same time, communications between Bead Water and the other Spanish settlements were to be cut. The Spaniards in each place would then be convinced that those in the others were destroyed and could not provide help.

Without benefit of calendar or clock, timing was precisely calculated to make possible a whole network of simultaneous, surprise attacks. Timing was also subtly adjusted to the weather, which in turn controlled the arrival of supplies that the Spaniards sorely needed.

Seldom have any oppressed people anywhere been better equipped with practical schemes for overcoming the obstacles that stood between them and their freedom. Rarely among the victims of the world's great empires has a leader like Popé appeared who could manage so amazingly to unite so many different and proudly independent peoples who spoke so many diverse languages.

By all accounts Popé, working in Red Willow, was the chief architect of this unity, but we have no information about exactly where he was after the planning was completed and the hour drew near for transforming his design for revolution into a reality.

Was the plan so perfectly conceived that it could now be carried out without any guiding intelligence at a command post? Perhaps, but it is hard to believe that Popé would not be near the center of events which could be the great achievement of his life.

These events began to follow each other with almost unbelievable rapidity, starting before daylight on August 9. The center of activity, the village of Dry Spot, was only nine miles from the main target—Bead Water—the Spanish capital. Dry Spot was also centrally located in relation to all the upriver villages. And it was at Dry Spot that runners—Catua and Omtua among them—were briefed in the predawn hours on August 9.

So it was that Catua and Omtua started on their run with cords that were knotted to announce that the rising would begin on August 13. And so it was that Catua and Omtua rendered a great service to all village Indians when they revealed that date before their young lives suddenly ended.

7/ Rebellion in the North

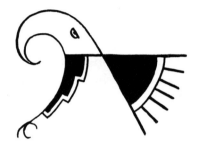

Eagle

All over the upriver country men put on war paint during the night of August 9. They stored new arrows in quivers they had made from mountain-lion skins. They took tough buffalo-hide shields down from the walls of their homes. In kivas they beat drums loud enough to help them feel ready for war, but not so loud as to tell the Spanish priests and soldier-farmers that war was coming.

In some villages, such as Grinding Stone, men wanted to do a prebattle dance, but could not because they had to keep secret the fact that they were going to war. (In this dance both men and

women took part. The men moved about, holding two lances decorated with painted gourds and
woven strips of cloth. The women, as a way of
wishing success and safety to the men, held ears
of corn, each decorated with two eagle feathers.)

These rituals had always gone on in the past
when war loomed. But now in each village the
War Chief and his assistants had to do the best
they could, lacking women, to prepare men for
battle. One practical thing the village military
leaders did was to divide the men into parties,
each with a special assignment. For example, one
party would be assigned to steal out in the dead
of night and go secretly to the Spanish farm
farthest from the village. Another would go off
in another direction to a big estate. A third party
would surround the house of the local magistrate
when there was such a house in the village. Still
another group of warriors would be ready to
attack the convent where the missionary and his
staff lived. In addition, patrols were assigned to
stop all traffic on the trails.

As the first daylight on August 10 began to
make jagged silhouettes of the peaks which the
Spaniards called the Blood of Christ Mountains,
Indians battered through the heavy doors and
shuttered windows of houses and convents.

The pent-up anger of decades burst out in one

devastating moment. With surging war cries, the Indians attacked and killed every Spaniard they found.

Many of the Spaniards—and the half-Spaniards who were called coyotes—were almost as poor as the Indians. Many had done little or no harm to the native Americans. Certainly the Spanish children were guiltless, but the rebel leaders had warned that there must be no exceptions if they were to convince Otermín that the revolutionaries meant what they said. So efficient were the war parties that only a very few Spaniards managed to escape. Five of these were from the upriver village of Red Willow.

In Red Willow, during the all-night secret ceremonies, men covered their bodies with paint. Each one used a design that was to his liking. Deep in the kivas there was a steady throb of music from drums. The War Chiefs gave final instructions; then, before dawn, men in small parties spread out over the countryside. When the sky was light enough so that they could see what they were doing, these flying squads attacked wherever a Spaniard lived. Very soon nearly every one of the seventy Spaniards around Red Willow was dead.

The moment the Spanish magistrate realized what was happening—and before he was killed

—he sent two messengers to Bead Water to ask for help. In the confusion these two men escaped, but not another Spaniard who had spent the night in Red Willow survived.

However, three Spaniards, Fernando de Cháves, Sebastián de Herrera, and one of his sons, were absent from Red Willow that night. Herrera, who had been born in Spain, had become a man of importance in New Mexico. It was his privilege to carry the royal banner which accompanied the governor wherever he went on official business. Recently Herrera had come from Bead Water to Red Willow with his wife and twelve children. He had then left his family, except for one son, in Red Willow and had gone into country where Ute Indians were camping. These Indians, who were nomads, had stolen many horses from the Spaniards over the years and now had a good supply. Possibly Herrera was hoping to buy back some of the stolen horses.

Whatever his mission, he was among Utes on the morning of August 10 when a rider—no doubt a Ute—galloped up from Red Willow with news that a revolution had broken out there. Herrera couldn't have been very far away when he received this news, and he and his companions started at once to see what was going on. As they approached the village, which lay at the foot of a great mountain, they could see the adobe houses built in two separate sections, each five stories high. Columns of smoke were rising, but not from the beehive ovens in which women baked bread outside their houses. The smoke came from the church and the convent. Both were in flames.

Men in Red Willow saw the Spaniards approaching. They rushed out to attack, and among them was the tuyo Francisco Pacheco. Although he had been appointed by the Spaniards, Pacheco—unlike some other tuyos—had agreed with Popé and Saca, and in the crisis he sided with his people against tyrants.

"We have killed the Spanish governor in Bead Water and his Secretary of War, Francisco Xavier," Pacheco told Herrera. That, of course, was a lie. "We have killed all the Spaniards here; now we intend to kill you." That was not a lie.

But Pacheco and the other men who had run out of the village were on foot, and the Spaniards were mounted. Not even the swift Apaches, who were now fighting alongside the Red Willow people, could catch the horses. The Spaniards got away. They headed south, avoiding the regular trails and roads, moving instead high along the mountainside. Behind them in Red Willow, the most northerly of the villages, more than three score of their countrymen were dead, including two missionaries and all the members of the families of Cháves and Herrera.

On August 10 at Dry Spot, nine miles from Bead Water, Obi and Nicolás continued the work of retribution they had begun the night before. In the early daylight outside the village, they met the missionary who lived there. He had spent the night in Bead Water and was coming now in hope that he could persuade the Christian Indians he knew to give up any thought they might have of rebellion. As an indication that he was not altogether sure of the loyalty of his parishioners, he had taken the precaution of carrying a big shield as he rode toward Dry Spot, and he also had a fully armed soldier who acted as his bodyguard.

The people of Dry Spot—all two hundred of them—were leaving their village when the priest approached. They were on their way toward the mountains, taking their own few cattle and many Spanish-owned animals with them. The priest hurried to catch them, and when he got close enough so that they could hear his voice, he urged them to return to their houses.

"My children, are you mad?" the missionary called out. "I will help you and will die a thousand deaths for you."

One death was enough for the people of Dry Spot. Obi and Nicolás met the priest in a ravine nearby. Soon Obi emerged from the ravine carrying the priest's shield. Nicolás, already covered with war paint, was now spattered with blood as well.

Other men grabbed the legs of the soldier and tried to pull him out of his saddle. The soldier's horse, terrified, reared, then charged away carrying his rider with him. Dry Spot men held onto the soldier as long as they could, but he got away.

Everywhere in the northern villages the story was much the same on August 10. Indians fell upon the priests, often in the churches. Just as the priests had destroyed Kachina masks, the Indians now hacked arms and legs off images. They seized silver chalices used in Catholic rituals. They destroyed crosses. And to show their utter rejection of the priests under whom they had suffered so much, many of the warriors spread their excrement on the altars.

The Indians left the bodies of priests where they fell; they deemed them unclean, unworthy of burial. In mockery, some of the warriors put on garments the priests had worn and jingled the little bells they had used during Mass. They climbed the church towers and rang the big bells in triumph. From some of the bells they took the clappers; others they dropped on the ground hoping to break them and silence them forever. In one church after another, the Indians piled straw and lit it with embers from the fires in their homes.

In isolated adobe farmhouses, war parties killed every man, woman, and child, then seized whatever they could use. Often they took cloth they had woven with their own hands or hides which they had tanned. They carried away corn they themselves had raised. Everywhere they seized cattle and horses and weapons. Soon many rebels were mounted, and before the day of August 10 was far advanced, a good number of Indians had put aside their bows and arrows. They now had harquebuses and swords.

That was true at Rose Trail, where everything went according to plan. In Water Gap the revolution was directed by one of Popé's most active colleagues, a man who was known to his neighbors as Little Pot. The Spaniards called him Ollita or Francisco.

Catiti, another close collaborator, finished the work of liberating his own upriver village of Kewa, then went on to lead the action in Sticky

Earth. There he was aided by a very old rebel leader who seems to have been half-Black. To the Spaniards he was known as Pedro Naranjo. No one recorded the name his Keres neighbors used for him.

Somewhere, apparently in the Tewa district, the military officer, Francisco Gómez, and some soldiers who were with him encountered a rebel Indian doing solitary patrol duty. Gómez, indicating his superior forces, urged the man to surrender in peace. The man refused, replying in Spanish that he would rather go to hell than surrender. The Spaniards promptly killed him, confident in the expectation that he would indeed go to the place of eternal damnation.

In Mountain Gap, where Tupatú had led in planning revolution, all the Spaniards were soon dead. The Indians had taken what they wanted from Spanish homes, and the hated church was in flames. This work of cleansing done, the men of Mountain Gap, following Tupatú, joined the men from Red Willow. Together these Tiwa-speaking people went south to join the Tewas in Popé's village of Grinding Stone.

Whether Popé was with them when they entered his old home, no one knows, but the chance seems good that he was there. He could hardly have remained aloof from the military action he had started. He must have been among the river of men that was growing ever larger as it flowed toward the capital at Bead Water, the seat of Spanish power.

In only two localities besides Red Willow in the upriver region did small groups of Spaniards survive. A few huddled in a farmhouse in a tiny Spanish settlement known as La Cañada. Several miles south of La Cañada a few others collected in a community called Los Cerrillos. Otherwise, except for the town of Bead Water, the upriver region was swept clean of Spaniards.

At Bead Water when dawn came on August 10, there was no sign of uprising. Nor had Popé and the other leaders planned to strike at that time at the Spanish capital where thick-walled government buildings surrounded large courtyards protected by heavy gates. An attack on this stronghold would be more effective—and less costly—when outlying Spanish settlements could not send help and when all Indian forces could be concentrated in one assault. Instead of a premature attack on Bead Water, the leaders chose to rely on a brilliant strategy which began to unfold that evening.

During the day of August 10 a handful of refugees from upriver had reached the capital with stories of terrible retribution. Others, fleeing from farms and towns to the south, had brought similar information. By nightfall a thousand people, very frightened and very uncomfortable, had crowded into the government buildings at Bead Water. Among this throng were Indians who pretended to side with the Spaniards but had really stayed on as spies. They, too, had an assigned task. They spread a rumor that all the Spaniards in and around the important Spanish stronghold at Kick Flint were dead.

This news greatly shocked Governor Otermín. He had been assured that some of the villages to the south were quiet and would not take part in the rebellion that Catua and Omtua had foretold. Kick Flint had seemed especially secure, and the governor had sent out word that Spaniards should use it as a place of refuge in case trouble did arise. Now, since no official word had come from Lieutenant Governor García whose headquarters were at Kick Flint, Otermín easily believed that the stronghold had indeed been destroyed.

What Otermín could not know was that García's messengers had been intercepted on the road. Moreover, at Kick Flint itself, another part of the Indians' grand plan was taking shape.

8/ Rebellion Far from the Center

Whirlwind

South and west of Bead Water the rising had not
gone quite so smoothly as in the north. Word
about the new date reached the villages a little
later than it did in the north. Not every attack
began at dawn. And so a good many Spaniards
were able to reach Kick Flint in accordance with
Governor Otermín's orders. Hurrying to the village by ones and twos and tens, they looked for
protection in its convent and church and behind
the thick walls of its houses.

Homes in Kick Flint already housed as many
Indians as could conveniently live there. People
were not happy about being obliged to make

space in their dwellings so that Spanish refugees could have shelter. Nor did they like being ordered to give up more of their precious food than they had already had to surrender as taxes to the king.

Friction developed. Many in Kick Flint, even those who had not felt much hope that revolution could succeed, resented the haughtiness of the Spanish refugees. Grumbling began and messengers who came from Popé found willing listeners. One bit of news in particular was talked about everywhere in the village, and the Spaniards heard it.

"All Metal People in the north have been killed. The governor and everyone in Bead Water is dead." So ran the rumor, just as the leaders of the revolution had planned.

Confusion and despair attacked the Spaniards, and these weapons cost the Indians no dead. The Spanish forces at Kick Flint would not be sent to aid the supposedly dead Otermín. And Otermín, equally deceived by the rumors in Bead Water, would think Kick Flint had been destroyed and would not make any plans that involved getting help from that quarter.

Meanwhile, in villages between Kick Flint and the capital, people rose and expressed their anger in many ways. At Dancing Place the little hand-

ful of retreating white men found only Indian
women left in the village. These women gave
them no comfort. "Our husbands have gone to
kill Spaniards," they shouted in Spanish.

At Melon Town the villagers stoned the doors
of the church. They removed images, vases—all
manner of religious objects—and desecrated the
altar. Then they piled straw in the church,
burned it, and quickly set off for a place in the
mountains where they could easily defend themselves in case of counterattack.

Runners did not arrive at the more distant
western villages until later in the day of August
10. At one of the two Hemiss villages an excited
messenger ran into the plaza at noon. There he
reported loudly that people everywhere had risen
in rebellion. He called on the Hemiss people, who
were nearly five thousand in number, to do like-
wise.

Without delay, Hemiss men moved against the
Spaniards. Soon the resident missionary in one
of the villages was dead. But from the other village the priest and an army officer and three
soldier-farmers managed to escape. Riding as
fast as they could, they kept ahead of pursuers
until they reached Scattered Hills. There another
priest had escaped death. He joined the fleeing
party which was now led by an officer sent out

by Governor Otermín to learn what was happening. As the little band of refugees rode on in terror, Indians, who until that day had been regarded as Christians, mocked their former masters and rang religious bells derisively to speed them on their way.

At White Rock, a village perched high on a cliff sixty miles west of Kick Flint, no Spaniard survived.

From White Rock runners carried a knotted cord still farther west to Zuni, announcing that the moment for revolution had come. Zuni men took down their shields, which were woven of yucca fiber or cotton cord. They armed themselves with stone knives and with clubs that some called "face smashers," and they killed the resident priest. Then they sent the knotted cord on to the Big Leggings (Hopi), who lived in the westernmost of all villages, and immediately moved out of their own Zuni villages and up onto Corn Mountain, where any avenging Spaniards who might appear would find it hard to reach them.

The story was a little different at Stone Top, the most easterly village, which got its name from the bare rock summit of a mesa on which it was built, about a mile from the Pecos River. On the mesa stood the most magnificent of all the churches in New Mexico. It was a huge building all plastered gleaming white, one hundred and seventy feet long, with six soaring bell towers. The missionary here had made many converts— so many that the Christians had built up a separate village between the old part of Stone Top and the church. In this new village there were no kivas, and from it had come many laborers and carpenters who worked on the construction of the church, following a style of architecture that came from southern France.

The Christian people at Stone Top became good artisans, but not one of them was ever sent to Mexico City to receive training for the priesthood. The missionary who had himself journeyed from the big city said the distance to it was too great for the men from Stone Top to travel.

Although the two thousand Indian people who lived at Stone Top were divided, there was sudden unity of Christian and non-Christian when on August 10 a runner arrived with a knotted cord. Soon the cleansing work began. Fire destroyed the great church, built by Indian hands but without a single architectural feature which had grown out of Indian life. Legend has it that men removed a bell from one of the high towers and carried it up onto the great mesa which rises south of Stone Top. There it could ring out, signaling freedom over a wide area.

Meanwhile, armed men continued to come together from other villages all over the upriver
country, gathering at prearranged collection
points. In the way in which springs flow into
streams, and streams join to make a river, a
mighty Indian army was assembling and moving
toward the capital.

And as night closed in on August 10, all the
women in upriver villages, and in some downriver villages too, did a dance they all remembered from the past. Slowly, sharing a common
hope, they wheeled, dancing for the safety of
their men who were away from home.

9/ Siege

Rain Cloud

The plans of the revolutionary leaders were working out very well, on the whole. Many of the warriors now had horses. Many were now armed with Spanish weapons. Traveling on foot or on horseback in groups of various sizes, they followed the trails that led to the capital.

Gradually the groups joined until two armies had assembled—one north of Bead Water, one south of it. On Tuesday, August 13, the southern army came in sight of the town. About nine in the morning it approached cornfields where Indian slaves from Mexico cultivated gardens. These slaves lived in a section of town called

Analco—a Mexican-Indian word which meant "across the river." The biggest building in Analco was San Miguel church, which had been built by Indian labor for the slaves to attend.

Governor Otermín, on the northern side of the river, watched in utter disbelief as five hundred Indian men, many mounted and many with Spanish arms, drew close. His astonishment grew when he saw who rode at the head of this army. It was Juan, the Indian servant he had trusted to carry messages of warning.

To advertise his commitment to revolution, Juan wore as a sash a large cloth bookmark used in the huge prayer book in the convent at Low Town. In his hand he carried two crosses, one red, the other white.

Juan, who had been a servant only a few days before, rode into the capital to confer—as one general to another—with Governor Otermín.

"If you will lead your people peacefully out of our country, you can all live," Juan said. "You can tell us that you choose life by taking this white cross from my hand. If you take the red cross, you will be choosing war and death."

Governor Otermín was furious. It was not in his nature to negotiate with a servant. He would not accept either cross. Instead he told Juan to return to his people and urge them to remain at peace.

Juan rode back and reported that Otermín had refused to leave. The warriors shouted down any talk of peace on the governor's terms. Again Juan rode into Bead Water. His second trip was no more successful than the first. Otermín could not believe that the Indians would force the Spaniards out of the colonial capital.

When Juan returned to his army the second time, the Indians broke into an uproar, blowing Spanish trumpets, ringing Spanish bells, and shouting for victory in three different languages.

The Indian leaders wanted to delay any attack on government buildings until the other great army of Indians arrived from the north. Then the two armies could close on the city the way the two jaws of a mountain lion close on a rabbit. This was the agreed-on plan. Meanwhile, warriors were directed to seize and fortify homes of the slaves in Analco. Someone in the army set fire to the nearby church of San Miguel.

Governor Otermín, hoping to intimidate the Indians, ordered a contingent of soldiers to draw up in battle formation outside the government buildings. With banners flying and arms glistening, the soldiers stood stiffly and waited. Noth-

ing happened. It was not part of the revolutionaries' plan to fight the Spaniards when and where
the Spaniards chose to fight.

A little later the Spaniards broke ranks and
managed to set fire to some of the homes in Analco, hoping thus to discourage any Indian ad-
vance through the settlement to the river and
across it into the capital.

The Indians remained where they were, but
only because they were still waiting for the army
from the northern villages. The safest place to
wait, they presently decided, was on the mountainside above the town. So they withdrew from
Analco, temporarily.

Next day, August 14, skirmishing went on
again in the southern part of town. And then,
near evening, the northern army appeared on a
hill just behind the government buildings.

With harquebuses they had captured from
Spanish soldiers, the Indians on the hill could actually fire down into a courtyard where hundreds
of Spaniards and their servants and their hundreds of horses and cattle and sheep milled
around.

Every Spaniard in the capital had moved out
of his home and into the continuous compound
of government buildings that surrounded several
large courtyards. Spaniards from some outlying

farms had also taken refuge here, along with the livestock they had brought with them.

Complete chaos was the result. The people had almost nothing to eat. The animals had absolutely nothing. Tension mounted steadily in the cramped quarters. It easily might have turned to panic if anyone had known what was going on downriver at Kick Flint.

Lieutenant Governor García, who had been away from Kick Flint on reconnaissance, returned on August 14. What he had seen upriver was utter devastation. And there was more devastation in the countryside around Kick Flint. Quickly, García called his most trusted advisers into conference. With one voice they recommended that he order the Spaniards to leave Kick Flint, where tension was obviously building, and go far to the south where the Indians were apparently quiet and might not bother them. At least by moving south, they would be closer to Mexico City.

It was illegal to order a retreat from Kick Flint —or from any other place in New Mexico. No Spaniard could leave the province without permission from Governor Otermín, acting as a representative of the Spanish king. And it was the king's firm intention that all Spaniards who entered New Mexico should stay there to defend his interests whether they wanted to stay or not. The Spanish colonists who denied freedom to Indians were themselves far from free.

But legal or not, García gave the order to retreat, and the Spaniards did leave Kick Flint. As they left, they saw evidence of destruction on farm after farm in the rich valley bottom. They also found that the Piro Indians, who a few years before had rebelled very bravely, were now thoroughly frightened and completely confused by what was going on. They had had no word from the rebel leaders. Now they had news only from the Spaniards who told only what it suited them to tell. And what the Spaniards said was that the revolutionaries would destroy them if they remained in their homes. As a result, the Piros decided to join the Spaniards in retreat.

On August 15 as the Spaniards fled southward from Kick Flint, the two Indian armies, one from the north and one from the south, began simultaneous attacks on the capital. About twenty-five hundred Indians, speaking half a dozen languages, took part in the assault. As the warriors moved in toward the center of town, they captured house after house. They turned each of these buildings into a fortress, sometimes by digging holes in the thick adobe walls through which they could shoot arrows or fire harquebuses.

Some of the houses the Indians captured went up in flames. So too did the big church which the Spaniards attended. Steadily the Indian army drew closer to the government buildings.

One long wall of the government headquarters faced on the plaza. On this side—the side where Catua and Omtua had been hanged—stood two fortified towers. In one of these was a chapel. The attacking Indians almost succeeded in setting fire to its doors. If they had burned their way through the chapel entrance, they could have entered the main buildings and overwhelmed the Spaniards by sheer force of numbers. But the fire did not eat through the thick wood of the great doors.

There was another crucial moment in the siege: Indians, wielding Spanish hoes and shovels, built a dam across the ditch which brought water to the government buildings. This was the only water supply for the thousand people and the hundreds of animals inside. Instead of reaching thirsty mouths, the water flowed on, close by but tantalizingly out of reach.

Babies began to cry. Women wailed. Cattle, aching from thirst, filled the air with their bawling. The bleating of sheep added to the din.

After only two days of siege, cattle, horses, and sheep began to die. People sickened.

Cries of triumph came closer and closer. Now

and then among the Indian shouts were derisive yells in Spanish.

"God, the father of the Spaniards, is dead," Indians called out.

"Santa María, mother of the Spaniards, is dead! Our gods have never died!"

In desperation, Governor Otermín decided that his only hope lay in making a sortie with as much show of strength as he could muster. Every one of his soldiers had been wounded. He himself had been shot twice in the face by arrows and once in the chest by a ball from a harquebus. But he had men who could still ride and horses that were still able to carry riders. To prepare for the sortie, priests said Mass. Then, accompanied on foot by a group of frightened slaves, who carried only bows and arrows, the small Spanish force burst out of the building with two cannon in tow. Above the soldiers, floated the royal banner, on one side of which was embroidered the image of Our Lady of Remedies. From dry throats came prayers to the Virgin Mary.

The Spaniards spurred their horses toward the Indians who were crowded together in the plaza in front of the government buildings. Taken completely by surprise, the Indians tried to get out of the way of the charging horses, but many died under their hooves.

The Spaniards rode on and set fire to the buildings in Analco where Indians had fortified themselves. Nearly three hundred of the revolutionaries died in the blazing traps. This wholesale death by fire accounted for a great part of the Indian losses in the siege of the capital.

As terrified survivors ran out of the burning buildings, Spaniards managed to capture forty-seven of them. Driving these prisoners along, they re-entered the government buildings. But before they closed the charred gates, they carried precious water into the crowded compound. This water gave immensely welcome, although temporary, relief to the miserable people huddled behind the thick adobe walls.

For a while there was relative quiet. Governor Otermín, still totally unable to understand what the Indians were doing and why they were doing it—and aching from three wounds—used the lull to question prisoners. After they had taken an oath as Christians to tell the truth and had given the sign of the cross, the Indians provided the governor no information from which he could take comfort. We do not know the exact words the prisoners used, but we do know that they gave thoroughly frightening details about the devastation in every outlying district.

When Governor Otermín had heard the testimony of the last of the captives, he ordered them all taken out in the plaza and shot. But shooting prisoners did not solve any problems for the beleaguered capital. It did not bring food or munitions, and there was no telling when the supply train, now long overdue, would arrive. Furthermore, the Indians set fire that night to every structure that was still intact outside the government buildings.

What could those in the capital do?

All of the officials met with Governor Otermín to discuss this crucial question. Very little talk was necessary. All agreed that they had to leave and move south, hoping to meet the supply train which was headed north. The supply train would have food and weapons and powder and shot. And the soldiers who accompanied the train could give them protection.

On the morning of Monday, August 21, a thousand frightened people made ready to start south. Some of the thousand were slaves so tied by bonds of habit and fear that they continued with their masters rather than make a break for freedom. Some were servants, not quite slaves, but also not quite free. Twenty of them, for example, were attached to one man, Francisco Gómez Robledo, the army officer who had arrested Catua and Omtua.

Most of the people would have to travel on

foot, carrying on their backs whatever belongings and supplies they could. For the thousand
refugees from the capital, there were only four
hundred horses and oxen, all weak from hunger
and prolonged thirst. For the wounded, there
were two wagons which they had to share with
government records (including testimony about
the rising) and other valuables the governor did
not want to leave behind.

Every man, woman, and child in the throng
feared that Indians in overwhelming numbers
would attack them once they were outside the
sheltering walls. Their utter helplessness would
be very apparent when they came into the open.
But with a kind of courage that matched their
desperation, the Spaniards filed out into the plaza
and beyond—and nothing happened. Absolutely nothing.

The revolutionaries did not attack. Their force
of more than 2,000 armed men merely looked on.
What they saw was a dream coming true. The
tyrants who had ruled over them for so long were
now leaving their land. There was no need to
risk even one more Indian life in a further attack.
It was enough to keep the Spaniards moving—to
make sure that they did not change direction and
try to return.

From every hilltop along the road to the south,
revolutionary warriors watched and showered

jeers down on the Spaniards, many of them bare-
foot, as they struggled to escape from the country
where they had once been masters.

Where was Popé at this time of triumph? The
Spaniards obviously did not know, and no Indians ever told. They left not a single record to
help us follow him as his plan was brought to
life. Was he high on a hill above Bead Water
where he could see all that was going on and
where he could send out orders as they might be
needed? We do not know, but there must have
been direction throughout the complex and well-
coordinated military operation of the revolutionary forces. No one of whom we have any knowledge could have acted in this capacity as well as
Popé.

While the combined Indian army watched the
retreat of the Spaniards, the revolutionary leaders knew that the supply train was still far to the
south. The twenty-four huge wagons that carried harquebuses and swords and saddles and
armor constructed of six layers of leather had
made slow progress from Mexico City. Now at
the ford across Big River they were completely
stalled. The river was in flood, and water spread
outward from it over the land. Mules and oxen
could not get the wagons across.

Finally, a report reached the leader of the supply train that all the New Mexico Spaniards who

survived a bloody revolution were coming down-river and were in dire need of help.

The retreating Spaniards, said the report, were in two separate groups. The nearest of these consisted of 1,500 refugees who had left Kick Flint on August 14. They had heard, just as Popé and his associates had planned, that the capital had fallen and all upriver Spaniards were dead. Without hope, without food or ammunition, they were dragging themselves to a ford near where the city of El Paso, Texas, now stands. Far behind, also headed for the ford, were the thousand refugees from Bead Water, still alive, contrary to rumor, but desperate.

The supply train, held up by high water, was much too late to give either group of refugees the support it needed if it was to stay in New Mexico. The careful weather-watching that Popé had done far to the north in Red Willow at the foot of high mountains was paying off. Heavy snows, plus a late spring, plus heavy summer rains were all adding up to freedom for people who believed in living in partnership with nature. For the Spaniards who had been determined to conquer both nature and man, there was only humiliating defeat, followed by years of life in hovels where the city of Juarez, Mexico, now stands.

10/ Freedom

Twinkling Star

When the warriors left their villages to take part in the siege of the Spanish capital, many women and children and old men moved out of their homes and went up onto mountains or mesa tops where they would be safe from enemy counter-attack if such should occur. Some women remained behind feeling sure that no Spaniard could survive. But wherever they were, at home or on mesa tops, the women again began dancing at night for the safety of their men.

After the Spaniards left Bead Water, there was a time for mourning, too. Men from every village had fallen in battle, and they were buried in the ancient way. In many villages it was thought proper to bury a dead man with his head toward the east. It was from the east that the life-giving sun rose each day.

Each fallen warrior was buried in his best clothes. His oldest male relatives clothed him and put his moccasins on the opposite feet. After death, these old men said, everything was opposite from the way it was in life. That was why the right moccasin must go on the left foot and the left moccasin on the right.

Four days after a warrior was buried, his relatives came to his home with food. They ate, and they offered food to sacred objects in the house. Also, they made offerings in the fields. All this giving was for the man who was no longer among them.

After the funerals were over, the old-time cycle of activities resumed, but not always exactly in the old way.

The people of Low Town, for instance, found new homes in the abandoned government buildings in Bead Water. The chapel there soon took on new existence as a kiva. Sacred shrines appeared on the four sides of the plaza, and Indians performed Kachina dances in the plaza which had been the scene of many executions and whippings of medicine men. Men wore Kachina masks which they had hidden from the Spaniards.

Celebrations went on throughout the liberated land. Popé, Saca, Little Pot, Catiti, Flat Nose, and other leaders visited every village. They rode from one place to another instead of walking as they always had before the revolution. Popé's mount was a big black mule.

The touring leaders urged people to wash in Big River, using suds made from the roots of the yucca plant. This was to cleanse them from all stain of Christianity. Indians should be completely Indian again.

Those who knew the Spanish language stopped using it. Those who had Spanish names gave them up and were known only by names which seemed right among their people. Every vestige of the Catholic religion was destroyed, or used in mockery.

In Dancing Place, Popé and the other leaders held a feast. As they sat at the large table around which the missionaries used to dine, the medicine men raised church chalices and proposed satiric toasts to one another.

"To your Paternal Reverence's health," Popé said according to an Indian who later reported to the Spaniards.

"Here is to your Lordship's health, Sir Governor," Catiti is supposed to have replied.

In Kewa the only songs heard in public for many years had been Catholic chants in Latin, which many Spaniards themselves did not understand. Now Kachinas once again raised their voices in songs, such as this one from the Keresan language:

> I, Deer Boy,
> Leave the home of the Kachinas
> Early in the morning
> To take care of
> The earth and the sky.
>
> I, Deer Maiden,
> Leave the home of the Kachinas
> Early in the morning
> To take care of
> The common people.

Throughout the land villagers also sang other songs—chants they had learned from the missionaries. But these they sang in ways that made them burst out laughing.

It was a good time in Aztlán. This Native American revolution had done what it had set out to do. It had driven tyrants from the land.

11/ A New Balance

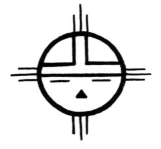

Sun God

The many Indian villages had not needed to be united before the well-armed Spanish invaders occupied their land. People did not do the kind of business with each other that required a central government to make laws and to enforce them. So, when the Spaniards left in 1680, the Indians felt that the need for unity had also gone away. Each village returned to governing itself. This was one part of the old way of life of which Popé did not approve. He preached the need for continuing unity.

No one knows the exact words Popé used, but they might have been something like these:

"Now that we have struck our great blow and driven the Metal People from our land, we must not think that they will vanish from the earth. The Metal People came once. They came like a river flooding our land, a river that is fed by a big spring and the melting of great snows. The river can flood again. We must continue to work together to protect ourselves from new flood waters."

Some of the leaders of the revolution agreed with Popé, but neither they nor Popé won much attention for their pleas for continued unity. The danger seemed too far away. Without an enemy visible and close at hand, the threats Popé talked about seemed unreal. It appeared obvious that the battle for freedom had been won.

Popé knew the nature of tyrants. He knew they would not give up an area as rich as Aztlán. But apparently about 1688, before he could persuade many people of the reality of the danger to which he pointed, Popé died. His wisdom died with him.

Although people had not seen the full importance of his last warnings, they mourned the leader who had done so much for them, and they buried him according to ancient ritual. At one point in the old ceremony a speaker addressed the body of Popé before it was placed in the earth:

"Now you do not belong here any longer. You belong with the Kachinas. Now you will have to help your people from the distant mountains and hills."

And the people soon needed help.

Having taken up their old separate ways, they began to think differently, even to act differently, and to quarrel. Some Keres, Tiwa, and Towa Indians began to be angry with Tewas. And as differences mounted, the Spaniards planned a new invasion. Because of their experience in the revolution, some former officials urged that not a single person who was even part Indian or part Black should ever be allowed to bear arms in New Mexico. In a document drawn up by the former members of the city council of the capital city were these words: "No Indian, half-Indian or mulatto may carry harquebus, sword, dagger or lance, or any other Spanish arms, nor may they own beasts or travel on horseback, the latter being permitted only to servants of soldiers on campaign or on the roads." Too many people who weren't pure Spanish, which really meant who weren't members of the privileged ruling class, had sided with the Indians against their masters.

The Spanish planners also knew that they must be very strong and very well armed. Most important, they should never again try to force village Indians to give up their ways.

As a result of this new policy, a kind of compromise was reached when Spanish raiders and soldiers came back very well armed in 1692 and succeeded in reconquering a disunited Aztlán. The Indians once again attended Mass in the churches of the Spaniards, but now they also openly entered their kivas and held dances in public. The revolution of 1680 had won much for the Indians. It had established a new balance along Big River. This is reflected in a story that some people tell to this day:

It seems that Po-Se-Ye-Mo and God had a contest to see which one was stronger. Po-Se-Ye-Mo won. Then after he had defeated God, Po-Se-Ye-Mo said to him, "I won the wrestling match, but you are really stronger."

And that's the way things have been in Aztlán. Strong native Americans and strong invaders have each had part of a victory.

After 1692, a new people began to appear in Aztlán. They are descendants of both the native Americans and the Spaniards, and Aztlán, where they have lived for nearly three hundred years, is their home as well as the home of Indians who still live there and still keep many of their ancient ways.

These new people, who are called Hispanos by some and Chicanos by others, bear no responsibility for the actions of Spanish rulers who invaded the area long ago. The Chicanos and the Indians have poverty as well as ancestors in common, and both are denied many privileges that English-speaking white citizens enjoy. Aztlán now provides prosperity only for a new wave of invaders who arrived long after the Spaniards had reconquered the land.

Perhaps one day a new Popé may help both Indians and Chicanos to become really free in the land where their dark ancestors were the very first settlers. Meanwhile, the nonwhite people who dwell along Big River are not simply waiting for a new Popé. They are finding ways to cooperate with one another as they begin to move toward control over their own lives—toward Red Power.

But that is another story.

Afterword

Some readers who have seen other accounts of what is often called the Pueblo Revolt of 1680 may wonder why the story in *Red Power on the Rio Grande* differs from the ones with which they are familiar. To these readers I owe an explanation.

Anyone who writes about the year 1680 in New Mexico must use as source material records prepared by the Spanish Governor Otermín and other civil and ecclesiastical officials. I have familiarized myself with these documents, which have been published. Also I have used anthropological studies of Pueblo cultures, and I have looked into what I could find of Indian history that has been interpreted from the Indian point of view. With Native American culture and outlook in mind, I have tried to re-evaluate the published summaries of the stirring events of 1680.

Most of these, including those which appeared while I was at work on my book, seemed to me to be history seen only through Spanish eyes. And none of the accounts seemed to me to make clear how great was the achievement of Native Americans when they ended Spanish imperial control in New Mexico. Indeed, one publication that has attracted some attention in historical circles plays down the Indian contribution to this successful Indian uprising. Fray Angelico Chavez in an article in the *New Mexico Historical Review* in 1967 seeks to prove that the real leader of the Indians was not Popé but a Black man who had come from the Valley of Mexico where he had gathered some knowledge of both Mexican-Indian and Spanish cultures. It is my belief that Chavez has made serious errors in his interpretation. He has underestimated both the grievances of the Indians and their capacity for asserting creative control over their own lives. Also he has mistaken for a Black man a Pueblo ceremonial dancer who wore a black mask.

There is no question that former slaves who

were wholly or partly African in ancestry did join the Pueblo Indians in their great move for freedom. However, there is no reason to think that an alien who had not received boyhood training in Pueblo culture could rise to eminence within a medicine society and then go on to become a leader over all leaders of all Pueblo medicine societies. Cultural barriers would make such a career impossible. Furthermore, the available evidence indicates that Popé was the most influential inspirer and director of the actions of the Pueblo Indians. I can see no reason to look beyond Popé for the "real" leader. Popé was the real leader, and a very great one, too.

Franklin Folsom

A Guide to Place Names

In the lefthand column are place names used in this book. In the column at the right are names for the same places as they are known today. If no equivalent name appears in the righthand column, the place has ceased to exist, at least on its original site.

Names used in this book	Names used today
Analco	Analco
Aztlán	The Southwest
Bead Water	Santa Fe
Big Leggings	Hopi
Big River	Rio Grande
Dancing Place	Santa Ana
Dry Spot	Tesuque

Names used in this book	Names used today
Grinding Stone	San Juan
Hemiss	Jemez
Kewa	Santo Domingo
Kick Flint	Isleta
La Cañada	. . . .
Los Cerrillos	. . . .
Low Town	Galisteo
Melon Town	Sandia
Mountain Gap	Picuris
Red Willow	Taos
Rising Leaf Lake	La Ciénega
Rose Trail	Santa Clara
San Cristóbal	. . . .
Scattered Hills	Zia
Sticky Earth	San Felipe
Stone Top	Pecos
Turquoise Town	. . . .
Water Gap	San Ildefonso
White Rock	Acoma
Zuni	Zuni

Pronunciation Guide

Acoma: AH-koma
Aztlán: ahs-TLAHN
Galisteo: gahl-iss-TAY-oh
Kewa: KAY-wah
Kiva: KEE-vah
La Cañada: lah kahn-YAH-dah
La Ciénega: lah see-EN-eh-gah
Los Cerrillos: lohs se-REE-yohs
Otermín: oh-tayr-MEEN
Picuris: pi-koo-REES
Popé: poh-PEH
Sandia: san-DEE-ah
San Juan: san HWAN
Taos: TOWSS
Tesuque: teh-SOO-keh
Tewa: TAY-wah
Tiwa: TEE-wah
Towa: TOH-wah
Tuyo: Too-YOH
Zuni: ZOO-nee or ZOON-yee

Sources

Bancroft, Hubert Howe
  1889   *History of Arizona and New Mexico, 1530-1888.* San Francisco: the History Company.
Bandelier, Adolph Francis, and Bandelier, Fanny Ritter, eds.
  1923- *Historical Documents Relating to New Mexico,*
  1937   Nueva Vizcaya, *and Approaches Thereto, to 1773.* Vol. 3. Carnegie Institution of Washington.
Bandelier, Adolph Francis, and Hewett, Edgar
  1937   *Indians of the Rio Grande Valley.* Albuquerque: University of New Mexico Press.
Chavez, Fray Angelico
  1954   *Origins of New Mexico Families in the Spanish Colonial Period.* Santa Fe: Historical Society of New Mexico.

1967 Pohe-Yemo's Representative and the Pueblo Revolt of 1680. *New Mexico Historical Review*, vol. XLII, no. 2.

Davis, W.W.H.
1869 *The Spanish Conquest of New Mexico*. Doylestown, Pennsylvania.

Dozier, Edward P.
1960 The Pueblos of the Southwestern United States. *Royal Anthropological Institute of Great Britain and Ireland. Journal*, vol. 90.

Forbes, Jack D.
1960 *Apache, Navaho, and Spaniard*. Norman: University of Oklahoma Press.

Gilbert, Hope E.
1940 Patriot of the Pueblos. *Desert Magazine*, vol. 3, no. 3.

Hackett, Charles Wilson
1912- The Retreat of the Spaniards from New Mexico
1913 in 1680, Beginnings of El Paso. *Southwestern Historical Quarterly*, vol. 16, no. 2; no. 3.

Hackett, Charles Wilson, ed.
1942 *Revolt of the Pueblo Indians of New Mexico and Otermín's Attempted Reconquest, 1680-1682*. Albuquerque: University of New Mexico Press.

Harrington, John P.
1920 Old Indian Geographical Names Around Santa Fe, New Mexico. *American Anthropologist*, N.S. 22, no. 4.

Horgan, Paul
1954 *Great River*, The Rio Grande in North American History. New York: Rinehart and Company, Inc.

Johnston, Philip
1956 When the Pueblos Rebelled. *Westways*, vol. 48, no. 5.

Josephy, Alvin M.

    1961   *The Patriot Chiefs. A Chronicle of American Indian Leadership.* New York: Viking Press.

New Mexico Historical Society

    1906   The Franciscan Martyrs of 1680. *Papers,* no. 7.

Ortiz, Alfonso

    1969   *The Tewa World.* Chicago: University of Chicago Press.

Parmentier, Richard J.

    1971   *The Mythological Triangle: Poseyemu, Montezuma, and Jesus in the Pueblos.* Senior Honors Thesis in Anthropology, Princeton University (entered at the Princeton University Libraries).

Parsons, Elsie Clews

    1929   The Social Organization of the Tewa of New Mexico. *American Anthropological Association Memoir,* no. 36.

Scholes, France V.

    1930-   The Supply Service of the New Mexican Missions
    1937   in the Seventeenth Century. *New Mexico Historical Review,* vol. V.

           Civil Government and Society in New Mexico in the 17th Century. *New Mexico Historical Review,* vol. X, no. 2.

           Church and State in New Mexico 1610-1650. *New Mexico Historical Review,* vols. XI, XV.

           Troublous Times in New Mexico 1659-1670. *New Mexico Historical Review,* vols. XII, XIII, XV.

Silverberg, Robert

    1970   *The Pueblo Revolt.* New York: Weybright and Talley.

Spicer, Edward H.

    1962   *Cycles of Conquest: The Impact of Spain, Mexico and the United States on the Indians of the*

  Southwest, 1533-1960. Tucson: The University of Arizona Press.

Twitchell, Ralph Emerson

  1911- *The Leading Facts of New Mexico History.* Vol.
  1917   I. Cedar Rapids, Iowa: The Torch Press.

  1925   *Old Santa Fe.* Santa Fe: New Mexico Publishing Corp.

White, Leslie A.

  1932   The Pueblo of San Felipe. *American Anthropological Association Memoir,* no. 38.

  1935   The Pueblo of Santo Domingo, New Mexico. *American Anthropological Association Memoir,* no. 43.

  1942   The Pueblo of Santa Ana, New Mexico. *American Anthropological Association Memoir,* no. 60.

Index

A

abalone shell, 61
Analco, 110, 111, 112, 117
anthrax, 50
Apaches, 30, 40, 42–3, 50, 74, 80–1, 96
area, size of, 75
armor, 43, 79, 84
Ash Youth shrine, 63
August 9, 21–34, 92–3
August 10, 35, 93–102
August 13, 109–12
August 14, 112–4, 121
August 15, 114-5
August 21, 118–20
Aztec Indians, 37
Aztlán, 37, 46, 79, 86, 125, 127, 129, 130

B

baby ceremony, 61–2
Bead Water (Santa Fe), 21, 23, 25, 47, 50, 57, 81, 86–7, 89, 91, 95, 101–2, 104, 110–3, 114–8, 120, 121, 122, 123
bear, sacred, 69, 71
Big Leggings (Hopi), 74, 86, 106
Big River (see also Rio Grande), 37, 69, 81, 84–5, 120, 124, 129, 130
birth ceremony, 60–1
Blood of Christ Mountains, 93
Blue Corn Woman, 60
Bua, Nicolás, 76–7, 88
burial ceremony, 48, 122–3, 127–8

C

Catholic (see missionaries)

Catiti, 76, 81, 85, 88, 99, 124
Catua, Nicolás, 21–34, 36–7, 91, 115, 118
ceremonies, 38, 39, 45–6, 47, 49, 53, 65, 67, 75, 122
  baby, 61–2
  birth, 60–1
  burial, 48, 122–3, 127–8
  confirmations, 64
  seven years, 63
  ten years, 64
Charles II, King, 36
Chato (see Flat Nose)
Cháves, Fernando de, 95, 97
Chavez, Fray Angelico, 132
Chicanos, 129–30
Christianity, 47, 56, 64, 107, 117, 124
Clemente, Esteban, 49
Cochise, 16
confirmation ceremony, 64
convicts, 44
corn, 38, 50, 60
Corn Mountain, 106
Coronado, 43
coyotes, 94
Crazy Horse, 16
Custer, 17

D

Dancing Place (Santa Ana), 104–5, 124
dialect, 40–1
documents, 16, 17, 37, 131
Dry Spot (Tesuque), 21, 23, 25, 30, 31, 34, 91, 97–8
Durán, Brother Andrés, 55

141

E

El Paso, Texas, 121
encomienda, 14
epidemic, 50, 53

F

Fallen Timbers, 18
famine, 50, 53
farmers, 42
farming, 38, 40, 42
feathers, 26, 46
feudal society, 45
Fine Society, 67
Flat Nose, 76, 81, 85, 124
Flint Society, 67
food, 38
forced labor, 15, 47
four, magic number, 65
Franciscan order (*see also* missionaries), 45
Francisco, 99

G

Galisteo, (*see* Low Town)
games, 62
Garcia, Alonso, 102, 113–4
gold, 43
Gómez Robledo, Francisco, 25, 100, 118
government buildings, 25, 111, 112, 115, 116–7
governor, Indian (*see also* tuyo), 22, 47
governor, Spanish, 23, 26, 55–6, 72, 86–7, 96, 131
Grinding Stone (San Juan), 57, 61, 63–7, 72, 74, 75–6, 77, 100
guns, 43, 81

H

hanging, 57
harquebus, 29, 79, 84, 112, 116

Hemiss (Jemez), 48, 74, 105
Herrera, Sebastián de, 95–6, 97
Hispanos, 129
Holy Thursday rebellions, 49
Hopi language, 41
Hopi people (*see* Big Leggings)
horses, 22, 25, 43, 79, 84

I

Inquisition, 15
Isleta, (*see* Kick Flint)
invasion by Spaniards, 42–4, 53–4, 128–9

J

Jemez, (*see* Hemiss)
Joseph, 16
Juan, 31, 110–11
Juarez, Mexico, 121

K

Kachina, 26, 52, 64–5, 66, 123, 128
Kachina masks, 49, 65, 66, 98, 123–4
Keres people, 74, 100, 128
Keresan language, 41, 125
Kewa (Santo Domingo), 76, 99, 125
Kick Flint (Isleta), 102, 103–4, 113–4, 121
king of Spain, 36, 44, 45, 113
kiva, 24, 56, 73, 76, 123, 129
knotted cord, 22, 28, 34, 87–8, 89, 106, 107
Kossa, 66

L

La Cañada, 101
La Ciénega, (*see* Rising Leaf Lake)
language, (*see also* Hopi, Keresan, Piro, Tewa, Tiwa, Towa, Zuni language), 26, 29, 31, 40–2, 75, 89
Large Marked Shield shrine, 63

leaders, secret, 47
legends, 38, 62–3, 67
Little Big Horn, 17
Little Kiva, 66
Little Pot, 81, 99, 124
looting for riches, 42–3
Los Cerrillos, 101
Low Town (Galisteo), 31, 110, 123

M

maize, 38
Manuelito, 16
masks, 49, 64–5, 66, 98, 123–4
medicine men, 45, 55–8, 64, 67–70, 72, 75
meditation room, 68–70
Melon Town (Sandia), 105
Metal People, 24
Mexico City, 50, 51, 107, 113, 120
midwife, 60
military duty, 45
missionaries, 44–6, 48, 49, 64, 97–9, 107, 124, 125
Misu, Diego, 28
Mountain Gap (Picuris), 76, 78, 100

N

Name Mother, 60–1
Naranjo, Pedro, 100
Navahos, 40, 48
Nicolás, 23–4, 34, 97, 98
northern army, 111, 112, 114

O

Obi, 23–4, 34, 97, 98
Obsidian Mountain, 63
Ollita, 99
Omtua, Pedro, 21–34, 36–7, 91, 115, 118
Otermín, Antonio de, 23, 25, 26–31, 86–7, 88, 102, 103–4, 110–11, 113, 116–9, 131

P

Pacheco, Francisco, 96
Pecos, (see Stone Top)
Pecos River, 106
Picuris, (see Mountain Gap)
Piro language, 41, 49
Piro people, 50, 77, 114
Plains Indians, 81, 85
plaza, 29–30, 65, 115, 116, 119, 123
Po-Se-Ye-Mo, 28, 70, 73, 129
Popé, 16–7, 57–8, 59–70, 71–82, 83–8, 90, 96, 120, 121, 124, 126–7, 130, 132
priest (see also missionaries), 48, 64, 107, 116
Pueblo Indians, 18, 43, 80–1, 131–3

R

raiding for food, 40, 43
record, written, 17, 36, 131
Red Willow (Taos), 48, 76, 78–9, 85, 90, 94–7, 121
religion (see ceremonies)
repartimiento, 15
Rio Grande (see also Big River), 37, 51
Ripe Squash, 61
Rising Leaf Lake (La Ciénega), 22
Rising Mist (see Po-Se-Ye-Mo)
ritual (see ceremonies)
Robledo (see Gómez)
Rose Trail (Santa Clara), 99
runners, 21, 31, 87, 89, 107

S

Saca, 16, 76, 78, 81, 85, 88, 96, 124
San Cristóbal, 21, 22, 25
Sand Creek, 18
Sandia, (see Melon Town)
Sand Lake, 63
San Filipe, (see Sticky Earth)
San Juan, (see Grinding Stone)
San Marcos, (see Turquoise Town)

San Miguel church, 110, 111
Santa Ana, (*see* Dancing Place)
Santa Clara, (*see* Rose Trail)
Santa Fe, (*see* Bead Water)
Santo Domingo, (*see* Kewa)
Scattered Hills (Zia), 105
serf, 45
seven-years ceremony, 63
Shimmering Mountain, 63
shrine, 63, 65
sipapu, 39, 56, 69
Situ, Pedro, 27
slaves, 43, 47, 51, 132
soldiers, 45, 46, 73, 97–8, 116–7
southern army, 109, 111, 114
Spider Women shrine, 63
spirit people, 39, 48
Sticky Earth (San Felipe), 99–100
Stone Man Mountain, 63
Stone Top (Pecos), 74, 106–7
Summer People, 39, 62, 63, 66
Sun-Water-Wind shrine, 63
supply train, 44, 50, 51, 53, 83–5,
    118, 120–1
swords, 43, 84

T

Tacu, 76
Tanoan language family, 41
Taos, (*see* Red Willow)
Tecumseh, 16
ten-years ceremony, 64
Tesuque, (*see* Dry Spot)
Tewa language, 26, 29, 31, 41, 57
Tewa people, 34, 72, 74, 100, 128
tithing, 14
Tiwa language, 41
Tiwa people, 74, 76, 100, 128
Towa language, 41
Towa people, 74, 128
town crier, 62

traders, 37, 75, 89
traitor, 25, 77, 88–9
Tupatú, 16, 76, 78, 81, 100
Turquoise Town (San Marcos), 22
Turtle Mountain, 63
tuyo, 22, 25, 47, 88, 96

U

underground spirit people, 39
Ute Indians, 95

W

wagon train, 44, 50, 51, 53, 83–5,
    118, 120–1
War chiefs, 22, 28, 31, 66, 80, 93, 94
War Society, 80
water, lack of, 113, 117
Water Gap (San Ildefonso), 55, 99
weather, 84, 90, 121
whipping, 57, 64–5, 72
White Corn Woman, 60
White Rock (Acoma), 46, 106
Winter People, 39, 63
witchcraft, 56, 72
women excluded, 66–7, 78
World Stretcher, 61
Wounded Knee, 18
written record, 17, 36, 131

X

Xavier, Francisco, 25, 78, 96

Y

yucca plant, 124

Z

Zia, (*see* Scattered Hills)
Zuni language, 41
Zuni people, 48, 106